T0358209

Cambridge Elements ≡

Elements in Contentious Politics
edited by
David S. Meyer
University of California, Irvine
Suzanne Staggenborg
University of Pittsburgh

BLACK NETWORKS MATTER

The Role of Interracial Contact and Social Media in the 2020 Black Lives Matter Protests

Matthew David Simonson
The Hebrew University of Jerusalem

Ray Block Jr.
The Pennsylvania State University

James N. Druckman
University of Rochester

Katherine Ognyanova
Rutgers University

David M. J. Lazer
Northeastern University

CAMBRIDGE
UNIVERSITY PRESS

Shaftesbury Road, Cambridge CB2 8EA, United Kingdom

One Liberty Plaza, 20th Floor, New York, NY 10006, USA

477 Williamstown Road, Port Melbourne, VIC 3207, Australia

314–321, 3rd Floor, Plot 3, Splendor Forum, Jasola District Centre, New Delhi – 110025, India

103 Penang Road, #05–06/07, Visioncrest Commercial, Singapore 238467

Cambridge University Press is part of Cambridge University Press & Assessment, a department of the University of Cambridge.

We share the University's mission to contribute to society through the pursuit of education, learning and research at the highest international levels of excellence.

www.cambridge.org
Information on this title: www.cambridge.org/9781009475709

DOI: 10.1017/9781009415842

First published 2024

A catalogue record for this publication is available from the British Library

ISBN 978-1-009-47570-9 Hardback
ISBN 978-1-009-41586-6 Paperback
ISSN 2633-3570 (online)
ISSN 2633-3562 (print)

Additional resources for this publication at www.cambridge.org/Simonson

Black Networks Matter

The Role of Interracial Contact and Social Media in the 2020 Black Lives Matter Protests

Elements in Contentious Politics

DOI: 10.1017/9781009415842
First published online: January 2024

Matthew David Simonson
The Hebrew University of Jerusalem

Ray Block Jr.
The Pennsylvania State University

James N. Druckman
University of Rochester

Katherine Ognyanova
Rutgers University

David M. J. Lazer
Northeastern University

Author for correspondence: Matthew David Simonson,
matthew.simonson@mail.huji.ac.il

Abstract: Scholars have long recognized that interpersonal networks play a role in mobilizing social movements. Yet, many questions remain. This Element addresses these questions by theorizing about three dimensions of ties: emotionally strong or weak, movement insider or outsider, and ingroup or cross-cleavage. The survey data on the 2020 Black Lives Matter protests show that weak and cross-cleavage ties among outsiders enabled the movement to evolve from a small provocation into a massive national mobilization. In particular, the authors find that Black people mobilized one another through social media and spurred their non-Black friends to protest by sharing their personal encounters with racism. These results depart from the established literature regarding the civil rights movement that emphasizes strong, movement-internal, and racially homogenous ties. The networks that mobilize appear to have changed in the social media era. This title is also available as Open Access on Cambridge Core.

Keywords: Social Movements, Protests, Black Lives Matter, Social Networks, Tie Strength

ISBNs: 9781009475709 (HB), 9781009415866 (PB), 9781009415842 (OC)
ISSNs: 2633-3570 (online), 2633-3562 (print)

Contents

1 Modern Social Movements

1.1 An Unprecedented Summer

Across the United States, the weekend of May 23–24, 2020, was politically tranquil. While coronavirus-related closures and the Memorial Day holiday allowed millions of Americans greater free time and flexibility, scarcely 0.001 percent of them appear to have taken part in protests. Of the forty-five protest events picked up by media outlets and documented by the Armed Conflict Location and Event Data (ACLED) Project, only a handful were recorded as having over a 100 attendees, the largest being a South Carolina boat rally in support of then-president Donald Trump.[1] Most others were protests against pandemic lockdowns or municipal development initiatives. A mere five were related to policing or racial justice, all of them local. These included two rallies in Georgia on behalf of Ahmaud Arbery, a Black Georgia man murdered by White vigilantes; a rally in Des Moines, Iowa, on behalf of DarQuan Jones, a Black man who was assaulted by White men shouting racial slurs; and two rallies outside of California prisons calling for the release of inmates threatened by COVID-19. Although protest activity had rebounded from its nadir in March, it still remained low relative to pre-COVID-19 pandemic levels. Few Americans appeared poised to take their discontent to the streets, despite grievances from the public health disaster, government-imposed lockdowns, and surging unemployment.

Then, on Monday, May 25, George Floyd, a forty-six-year-old Black father, was brutally murdered by Minneapolis police officers during an arrest attempt before a horrified crowd of onlookers. Several witnesses, who pleaded with the police to desist, recorded the murder on their phones and uploaded the recordings to social media. The next day, a Tuesday, seven protests associated with the Black Lives Matter movement appear in the ACLED dataset. The number tripled on Wednesday, then tripled again the following day. The weekend of May 30–31 saw 856 ACLED-confirmed protests, 95 percent of which were associated with the Black Lives Matter movement. The movement reached its zenith the following weekend, June 6–7, with 1,212 ACLED-confirmed protests across all fifty states, hundreds more in cities around the world, and an untold number of others overlooked in reports amid the flurry of protest activity. Though protest turnout is notoriously difficult to estimate, surveys indicate that between 6 and 7 percent of American adults attended a protest (AP-NORC Center 2020; Parker, Horowitz, and Anderson 2020), rates not seen since the

---

[1] Armed Conflict Location and Event Data are systematically human-coded based on media, social media, government, and non-governmental organization reports, and local partner organizations. For more information, see https://acleddata.com/#/dashboard and Raleigh et al. (2010).

1960s–1970s, if ever (Buchanan, Bui, and Patel 2020). Our survey, described in later sections, arrived at a slightly lower turnout rate (4.5 percent of American adults). Even so, this suggests that, at a minimum, over ten million American adults attended a Black Lives Matter protest.[2]

The 2020 protest wave also was remarkably diverse. Despite being portrayed in the media as a left-wing movement, our data reveal that the protests also included millions of Republicans (19 percent), Trump supporters (20 percent), and conservatives (13 percent). Among adults, protesters tended to be young (45 percent were under 30), though about a fifth were over forty-five. Adults with graduate degrees were overrepresented (21 percent),[3] yet another 28 percent had never been to college. Although urban protests grabbed the media spotlight, protesters also lived in predominantly suburban (50 percent) and rural (9 percent) counties. Most striking of all, however, was the extent to which the protests' racial makeup reflected that of the nation as a whole, rather than the group that was the focus of the protests. Though exact numbers vary by source, all surveys of the 2020 protests agree that the majority of protesters were *not* Black. In our survey, we found that 52 percent of protesters self-identified as White, similar to Chenoweth et al. (2022) (55 percent), Fisher (2020) (54 percent), and a Pew Research survey (46 percent).[4] Black people made up around 20 percent of protesters according to our survey, one-and-a-half times their share of the population, while Hispanic Americans were slightly overrepresented, and those identifying as Asian or other were close to their population share.

Not only were the 2020 BLM protests likely the largest protest movement for any cause in American history (Buchanan, Bui, and Patel 2020), but they were also far more racially diverse than the 1960s civil rights movement (Fisher 2020; Morris 2021; Washington 2020). According to civil rights and social movements scholar Doug McAdam,

> While the '60s movement benefited at times from considerable white support, the levels of actual protest participation by whites was minimal. … there were sympathy demonstrations in the North in support of the sit-ins, and considerable white financial support for the major civil rights organizations, but very little in the way of active white participation in the major Southern campaigns. (McAdam 2020)

---

[2] While we will use "Black Lives Matter" or "BLM" as a shorthand, we acknowledge that not everyone who protested police violence or racism used that slogan, nor were all of them associated with organizations like the Black Lives Matter Global Network or the Movement for Black Lives.

[3] In our full survey sample of American adults, weighted to match the US census, 13 percent had a graduate degree; among those attending BLM protests, 21 percent did.

[4] www.pewresearch.org/social-trends/2020/06/12/amid-protests-majorities-across-racial-and-eth nic-groups-express-support-for-the-black-lives-matter-movement/.

At the same time, the Black Lives Matter movement itself was not nearly so widespread and racially diverse before the summer of 2020. In one sense, the Black Lives Matter movement was born in July 2013, when racial justice activist Alicia Garza coined the phrase in a Facebook post, fellow activist Patrisse Cullors responded to the post with the hashtag #BlackLivesMatter, and another activist, Ayọ (formerly Opal) Tometi, purchased the www.black livesmatter.com domain name (Chotiner 2020). And yet, although the immediate impetus for the phrase was the acquittal of George Zimmerman in the murder of Trayvon Martin, in another sense, the movement had already been around for years. According to Garza (2021), the new label simply brought together activists and organizations who had long been working on racial justice, incarceration, police brutality, and related issues. Wherever one places the founding of the movement, before the 2020 protests the movement's leadership and participants had been overwhelmingly Black (Fisher 2020; McAdam 2020). Moreover, while the movement had been through cycles of rapid growth – such as after the killing of Michael Brown by police in Ferguson, Missouri, in 2014 – the 2020 wave of protests was of an entirely different order of magnitude.[5] How did participation in the movement grow so rapidly? And how did the movement draw in so many people from beyond its previous base of veteran social justice activists and Black people?

Some of this protest attendance (or "turnout") almost certainly stemmed from the COVID-19 pandemic, which generated both grievances to protest and the free time or flexibility to do so. Protesters were far more likely than non-protesters to have started working from home, had their school closed, have a member of the household diagnosed with COVID-19, lost their job or suffered financial setbacks, had problems working from home, or endured problems with childcare (Lazer et al. 2021). Furthermore, in addition to George Floyd's murder, the pandemic generated outrage due to the virus' human and economic toll, anger at authorities for lockdown measures, and a pent-up desire to leave one's home and socialize (Arora 2020). Yet, the pandemic also threw up substantial barriers to attending. With a vaccine still months away and the risk of outdoor transmission still uncertain, attending a protest posed an unknown level of risk to both protesters and their families. Moreover, opportunities for in-person recruitment – whether in a school cafeteria, over an office water cooler, or on a night out with friends – were drastically curtailed. In short, the pandemic itself may have made people more angry and available enough to protest, but it could not in itself provide the sort of coordination needed to bring them together. Something else would be needed to notify potential protesters of

---

[5] For further context regarding the movement's evolution, see Brown, Block Jr., and Stout (2020).

demonstrations happening nearby, convince them that other people would actually show up, and persuade those on the fence to come along. That something, we argue, was social networks – the sum total of human relationships forged both in-person and on social media. In particular, "Black networks" – the ties linking Black people to non-Black people and one another – and online networks – thanks in part to the consequences of COVID-19 – were to have an unprecedented impact.

1.2 Studying Movement Mobilization

Mass social movements play a critical role in politics by highlighting points of contention and stimulating cultural and policy change (see Browning, Marshall, and Tabb 1984; Gause 2022a; McAdam, Tarrow, and Tilly 2001). Exactly how movements emerge is a tricky question: only those that occur are observed, and there exists considerable heterogeneity across movements. Nevertheless, although people's motivations and the nature of their participation may differ, they must at some point in the process (a) be persuaded to participate and (b) be informed when and where to do so. We refer to these two actions as mobilization. The mobilizing force may be a charismatic leader, an existing organization, or reports on the nightly news that galvanize people into action. In particular, scholars have long pointed to social networks – both face-to-face and online – as an important driver of mobilization (see, e.g., McAdam 2010; McAdam, McCarthy, and Zald 1996; Morris 1981; Morris and Herring 1987). Network mobilization, we find, was particularly influential in the 2020 Black Lives Matter protests. While Black Lives Matter organizations and leaders played an important role in organizing protest events, social networks provided the megaphone to broadcast their existence to a mass audience. Our focus, thus, is on "last-mile mobilization" – the final steps needed to bring together a large number of individuals to a given protest event. We also examine the role of networks one step earlier in the process – persuasion – while acknowledging that social ties are one factor among many (e.g., the pandemic, lockdowns, and graphic video of George Floyd's murder) that convinced people to protest.

Our research design centers on a survey in which we asked people if they attended a protest, why they did so, and to whom they spoke about it. Since these questions were part of a much larger survey of Americans about life during the pandemic, we are also able to compare the personal networks and demographic traits of those who protested to those who did not. Rarely has a single study been able to address all of these questions with one sample. Typical nationwide polls of roughly 1,000 people can inform us about the differences between protesters and non-protesters, but since they include at most a few dozen protesters, they are too small to draw inferences about why different types of people protested. Surveys fielded in-person at protests can address the latter, but they generally lack a comparison group of non-protesters. In our case, we were fortunate to have access to a massive sample of approximately 20,000–25,000 respondents each month from June to December 2020 through the COVID States Project. Combined with a protest movement that mobilized over 4 percent of the adult population, this approach allows us to collect data from over 5000 protesters and over 100,000 non-protesters, more than enough to explore variations among the protesters themselves and draw comparisons to everyone else. This is, to our knowledge, the largest general population survey of protester behavior ever conducted and, as such, has the potential to offer new insights into BLM in particular and protest mobilization writ large.

That said, it is important, from the start, to note the limitations of our approach. First, the size of the sample is made possible by the fact that we draw on existing online panels of paid respondents, a far less expensive approach than traditional telephone surveys. Rather than probability sampling (e.g., randomly selecting phone numbers to call), this approach relies on quota sampling (setting a quota for each race, gender, etc.) and reweighting (giving more weight to respondents from under-sampled groups) to match the proportions of each group reported in the census. As detailed in Section 3, there is substantial evidence suggesting that population estimates obtained from the COVID States Project's align with those from traditional surveys – and, more importantly, with "ground truth" administrative data such as vaccination rates. Nevertheless, these respondents may differ in important ways. For instance, paid respondents may be less attentive to the questions they are answering than those who volunteer their opinions for free. Unpaid volunteers, on the other hand, may be more likely to volunteer their time for a cause, thereby inflating traditional surveys' estimates of protest turnout. This may explain why other surveys about BLM found a slightly higher turnout rate than ours did.

Second, in contrast to "whole network" surveys that capture all the individuals in a community and the ties between them, an "egonet" survey such as ours captures isolated samples of the larger network. We asked respondents about their friends and acquaintances, but we had no way of learning about their friends-of-friends or how many links apart respondents are from one another. Thus, we cannot trace the spread of viral videos or posts across the entire network, nor can we determine who lies at the center of the network and who is on the periphery. At times, this limitation prevents us from distinguishing between rival explanations, and we acknowledge as much.

Our focus is on mobilization for a *specific protest event*, not mobilization into the movement per se.[6] In so doing, we sidestep the tricky question of what exactly constitutes membership in a decentralized movement where most participants are not card-carrying, dues-paying members of a particular organization.[7] Instead of asking "who is a member?," we picture each respondent as being located somewhere along an insider-outsider spectrum. At one end, we find the movement's founders and their inner circle – the ultimate insiders. Next, come longtime activists in the movement, then sporadic protest attendees, then people who have protested for related causes but not the movement at hand. At the far end, we find people who have never protested at all. For this study, we divide the insider-outsider spectrum into three categories:

(1) insiders: those who had previously attended a racism/police violence protest
(2) ambiguous: those who had previously attended protests but only for other causes
(3) outsiders: those who had never attended a protest

In our analysis, we focus on the contrast between the first and third categories. Moreover, in keeping with the spectrum proposed above, if a respondent reported being mobilized by an organization, protest organizer, or activist, we say they were mobilized by an insider. A key question of this study is whether outsiders tended to be mobilized by insiders or by fellow outsiders.

Our findings are threefold. First, we examine tie strength, finding that weak ties (e.g., acquaintances) have a far larger impact on protest mobilization than strong ties (e.g., close friends and family). While earlier work has given considerable attention to personal recruitment – and this sort of recruitment did indeed rely heavily on strong ties – far more protesters attributed their turnout to seeing posts on social media, a medium dominated by weak ties.[8] Second, we explore how social network ties affect insiders and outsiders differently. Contrary to the usual paradigm of insiders drawing their outsider friends and family into their movement, we found that outsiders' mobilization did not depend on access to insiders but could just as easily be driven by ties to victims of racism and police violence, regardless of their insider/outsider status. Third, cross-cleavage ties – ties spanning the social cleavage between Black people and non-Black people – played a decisive role in driving non-Black participation. Both integrated neighborhoods and interracial friendships

---

[6] To wit, we do ask respondents whether this was their first protest (and if it was their first protest about racism/police violence) but not whether they had already been involved in BLM in other ways.

[7] Likewise, we avoid having to decide whether movement membership ought to be defined by the researcher, social movement organizations, or the participants themselves.

[8] Including online followers whom the user has never met. While some studies might classify these individuals as strangers rather than weak ties, we include them as "weak ties" since they maintain a communication link that can be used for mobilizing.

were instrumental in mobilizing millions of non-Black Americans to fight for the rights of Black people.

These findings are important to understanding what may turn out to be a pivotal moment in American race relations – and indeed, in American politics generally. The 2020 BLM protests were, cumulatively, an event that shifted the national conversation about racism and policing and helped achieve widespread policy change at the state and local level (Dunivin et al. 2022; Ebbinghaus, Bailey, and Rubel 2021; Mazumder 2019; Peay and McNair 2022). Our study shifts the spotlight from the role of organizations, leaders, and activists – so often given credit for turning out "the masses" – to the role of ordinary participants and victims of police violence/racism in mobilizing one another. If the social fabric of the nation is ultimately transformed by these protests, it will be due in part to the ability of Black people to draw on the social fabric that already existed – that is, their personal ties, particularly those to other races. The potential success of Black Lives Matter, therefore, owes a debt not only to the organizers who built up the present movement over the past decade but to the civil rights activists, lawmakers, and citizens who worked to integrate Americans' neighborhoods, schools, and social networks over the past three-quarters of a century.

Beyond this historical event, our findings contribute to broader theories about social movements by examining what parts of those theories may have changed – or shifted in importance – in the social media era (Heaney 2022). This is not to say that Black Lives Matter in 2020 is necessarily typical of a new type of social movement. The circumstances of the pandemic were unique. Authors such as Tufekci (2017) and Fisher (2019) offer a wider perspective by comparing multiple protests in recent years. However, while the 2020 protests may be exceptional, they are certainly not obscure. Given the speed with which the movement spread to other countries, it seems highly likely that organizers of other social movements are already drawing lessons from the 2020 protests, much as Martin Luther King Jr. drew inspiration from the protests of Mahatma Gandhi. Whether they draw the right lessons and succeed in adapting them to new contexts remains to be seen. Thus, we expect many of our discoveries will find echoes in future movements, both in successful mobilizations and in mobilizations that flounder due to contextual differences that organizers had not foreseen.

On that note, we now examine the specifics of the 2020 BLM protests to better understand the scope conditions of our findings.

1.3 Generalizability of the BLM 2020 Protests

What are the defining features of the 2020 protests? How might these features affect the generalizability of our findings? Four elements of the 2020 BLM movement strike us as particularly relevant: its antiracism agenda, the role of social media, a non-hierarchical leadership structure, and its intersectionality. First, it was an *antiracist* movement for a marginalized Black population that has long experienced mistreatment by the state, most pointedly (at the time) as victims of unjust police killings. This defining feature underscores the important role that pre-existing social identities can play in social movements more generally (see Stryker, Owens, and White 2000). Our findings may therefore be most applicable to movements that seek to advance the rights of a downtrodden group with extensive ties to the rest of the population. A group that is relatively isolated within the broader social network due to speaking a different language or living exclusively in one province would likely have a harder time building allied support through cross-cleavage ties. Similarly, many respondents reported being motivated by contacts sharing personal stories about being victimized by racism or police violence (see Section 6). A movement without victims who can share their stories (e.g., save the whales) would not benefit from this mobilization pathway.

A second distinctive feature of the 2020 protests was the integral role of social media. Social media was already a central feature of Black Lives Matter prior to 2020 (Carney 2016; Cox 2017; Jackson, Bailey, and Welles 2020; Mundt, Ross, and Burnett 2018). More than nearly any other American mass movement, Black Lives Matter has made successful use of online platforms for recruitment and publicity. Moreover, the hashtag #BlackLivesMatter served not only as a practical tool for spreading the word but as a locus for the formation of a new social identity and community (Ray et al. 2017). In this sense, it fits well with what Earl and Kimport (2011), Gause (2022b), and others refer to as a "digitally enabled movement." Such a movement turned out to be particularly well suited to the conditions created by the COVID-19 pandemic. With other forms of social interaction curtailed, Meta – the parent company of Facebook, Instagram, and WhatsApp – reported a substantial increase in messaging across all three platforms (Schultz and Parikh 2020). Thus, not only were there fewer opportunities for traditional forms of protest mobilization (e.g., face-to-face recruitment, overhearing other people's conversations, flyers in public places), but mobilizers utilizing social media also had a far larger audience than usual.

What does this mean for other movements? On the one hand, the pandemic's abatement might lead to a resurgence of traditional forms of face-to-face recruitment and offline modes of publicity. However, the pandemic may have permanently transformed social relations, with Americans moving out of cities and more employers permitting employees to work from home (Whitaker 2021), thereby curtailing opportunities for offline mobilization. At the same time, social media usage grew dramatically during the pandemic (Einav 2022) and seems unlikely to decline in the near future. Thus, it seems probable that the patterns of digital mobilization we observe in BLM 2020 will continue, though their importance may vary from one movement to the next.

A third key characteristic of the 2020 BLM protests was the movement's unconventional organizational structure. As its founders and activists acknowledge, BLM is not a tightly structured organization (Tometi and Lenoir 2015). While leaders of organizations such as Black Lives Matter and the Movement for Black Lives made important contributions by scheduling events and notifying supporters through social media, the role of formal organizations was not nearly as prominent as it has often been in past movements. For example, the civil rights movement of the 1950s and 1960s was organized in a more top-down fashion, employing a "standard" template of tried-and-true processes to mobilize participants while shaping national-level narratives (Lee 2002). This included reliance on local organizations such as churches and student groups, and national organizations such as the Southern Christian Leadership Conference to mobilize and recruit members. Both the top-down and decentralized models of organizing continue to be employed in the twenty-first century (Imperial 2021). Although we expect our findings to be more relevant to decentralized movements like BLM, top-down movements also benefit from informal, pre-existing networks (e.g., McAdam 1986).

Fourth, BLM's theme of intersectionality distinguishes it from many past movements, including the mid-twentieth-century civil rights movement, and may have shaped its patterns of mobilization. A common refrain in BLM activist circles is that it "ain't the movement our parents or grandparents experienced" in the 1960s (e.g., Checco 2018; Edgar and Johnson 2018; Green et al. 2016; McGlone 2016). The movement was founded by three Black women, two of whom self-identify as queer, and insiders have, from the get-go, espoused an intersectional vision that centers all Black lives, including but not limited to, Black women, femmes, and queer and trans folk (Fisher and Rouse 2022; Jackson 2016; Smith and Bunyasi 2016).[9] Garza (2021), one of these founders, summarizes this desire for movement inclusivity eloquently in the following passage: "We had to bring people together and advocate for ourselves, ... to build that movement, we have to go about the task of building bases – ever expanding groups of people organized around our vision of change."

BLM insiders have sought to set the movement apart from religiously grounded, cisgender, heteronormative notions of liberation while rejecting essentialist ideas of "respectability" that often exclude women and LGBTQ

---

[9] Garza (2021, 266) speaks directly in her memoir about the need for BLM to "learn the right lessons" from past movement efforts for racial equality and to move beyond patriarchal, heteronormative, and respectability-politics-based notions of racial advocacy.

groups from conversations about racial justice (Board et al. 2020; Bunyasi and Smith 2019; Cohen and Jackson 2016; Jefferson 2018). As an intersectional movement, Thompson (2020, 241) notes that BLM represents an "example of the transformational potential of social movements to challenge the societal ideas about race, gender, and class that simultaneously hide and solidify hierarchical relationships of political power."

Movements that espouse intersectionality are well positioned to facilitate mass mobilization through social media and cross-cleavage ties. A movement that seeks to evade extant power structures will likely embrace nontraditional channels of recruitment such as using social media rather than relying on established opinion leaders (e.g., religious or partisan leaders). It also may be more welcoming to outsiders, if the "right" messages are chosen (Bonilla and Tillery 2020) that appeal to multiple identities, including those from other marginalized populations (e.g., trans individuals). In this sense, an intersectional framing could make the movement more inviting to non-Black people who share one of those other identities. This elevates the importance of cross-cleavage ties, for instance with Black trans people reaching out to recruit non-Black allies from the trans community. As will become clear throughout the Element, these types of ties proved vital for the 2020 protests.

All told, while BLM is certainly distinctive, it is not so unique as to render our findings inapplicable to other movements. We expect that our findings will be most relevant to movements that share some or all of the following features: (1) a victim group that is not too isolated from the rest of the country, (2) taking place in the social media era, (3) a decentralized structure, and (4) a commitment to intersectional inclusion. However, these features exist on a spectrum along which movements may be more (or less) similar to BLM, and no one of them is a prerequisite for all our hypotheses. Thus, we expect our findings to hold relevance for a broad range of movements.

In the next section, we lay out the empirical puzzle to be addressed and situate our three hypotheses – about tie strength, insider/outsider status, and cross-cleavage ties – in the wider literature.

2 The Ties That Mobilize

2.1 Mobilization and Social Network Ties

A crowd of demonstrators parades down Main Street, chanting slogans in unison and carrying homemade – and yet remarkably similar – signs. How did these people come to be marching in the same place at the same time? Why do so many of them already know one other? Why are these individuals out here marching, while other people who support the same cause remain home?

Part of the explanation for knowing one another surely lies in homophily – people tend to befriend and marry those with similar values (McPherson, Smith-Lovin, and Cook 2001). Variation in who actually shows up can be explained, in part, by who is likely to have the time or flexibility to attend (Petrie 2004) or believes they are capable of making a difference (e.g., Bolsen, Druckman, and Cook 2014; Lubell, Zahran, and Vedlitz 2007). Yet, acting on a belief requires more than attitudes, availability, or identification with the cause (Coleman and Ostrom 2011; Olson 1965). What spurs a latent supporter to action? How do they learn when and where to show up? Why demonstrate on behalf of a particular marginalized group when there may be multiple causes they identify with and multiple groups they care about?

We cannot address these questions adequately without considering the social motivations for protesting. Relationships with organizers, activists, or victims – while not necessarily sufficient to change the mind of an opponent – may prove crucial in swaying a fellow supporter to get off the couch and into the street. Social factors, most directly via mobilization, can explain how mass action comes to be so well-coordinated or why we find protesters clustered together within the broader social network. Although intrinsically motivated individuals are perfectly capable of seeking out opportunities for political action on their own accord, they are even more likely to get involved if someone else urges them to do so – that is, if they are mobilized (Castells 2015; Porta and Diani 2020). For others, encouragement from role models or peers prompts them to take actions they would never have otherwise considered or prioritized (Campbell and Wolbrecht 2020).

Mobilization solves both a *collective action problem* – an individual who stays home will still benefit from whatever changes the protesters achieve – and a *coordination problem*, in which would-be protesters must agree on a time and a place for action (Crossley 2002; Diani and McAdam 2003; Diekmann 1985; Gamson 1992; Hardin 1982; Olson 1965; Schelling 1960). Without dismissing the relevance of other factors – such as attitudes, identity, and efficacy – our goal is to unravel the complexity of mobilizing movements. An initial distinction concerns the identity of those doing the mobilizing. A common framing takes the perspective of elites seeking to mobilize the masses, whether for an electoral campaign, strike, demonstration, or rebellion. Leaders can either use "direct mobilization," contacting the supporters through their organizations, campaign staff, and volunteers, or they can rely on "indirect mobilization," allowing recruitment to spread organically via word of mouth through neighbors and friends (Gerber and Green 2000; Gerber, Green, and Larimer 2008; Rosenstone and Hansen 1993).

This terminology works well for electoral campaigns but is ill-fitting for so-called leaderless movements such as the 1989 Leipzig protests in East Germany

(Opp and Gern 1993), the Tea Party, Occupy Wall Street, the pro-democracy movement in Hong Kong, and the early stages of the Arab Spring. Although formal organizations and leaders played a part in these movements, to call their mobilization efforts "direct," in contrast to "indirect" mobilization outside their control, would be to place these organizations and leaders at the center. In contrast, many of these organizations are themselves the byproduct of ordinary people mobilizing one another and then coming together to coordinate their efforts, forming new groups and rallying around new leaders. When existing organizations and leaders have gotten involved, they have contributed to or, in some cases, co-opted these movements (see also Morris 2000). However, from the point of view of the original citizen mobilizers, their own efforts going door to door (or tweet to tweet) doubtlessly seem more direct than would mobilizing their friends and neighbors through an outside organization. We thus differentiate *personal motivations* to protest (e.g., attitudes, identity), *organizational motivations* (e.g., recruitment by insiders tied to the movement), and *socially networked motivations* (e.g., mobilization by social media posts).[10] The decentralized nature of the BLM organization makes socially networked motivations more relevant. As mentioned, BLM's founders themselves acknowledged it to be a "leaderless movement" model (Tometi and Lenoir 2015). Socially networked or interpersonal connections, we predict, will be far more important than organizational efforts in explaining how millions of Americans found themselves assembled in large groups across the nation, calling for police reform and racial justice.

The question, then, for us is how exactly networks worked and, specifically, which social networks proved most vital in the summer 2020 protests. In exploring that line of research, we contribute to the long-standing multi-disciplinary work on social networks and protest mobilization (e.g., Diani and McAdam 2003). Scholars have long recognized that the social structure of communities and societies (i.e., networks) is a crucial factor in the rise of mass movements and rebellions (Oberschall 1973; Passy 2001; Zhao 1998). These social structures not only facilitate collective action (Olson 1965) and lower the costs of involvement (Kuran 1991), but they also offer benefits in their own right, such as the pleasure in coming together to fight for a common goal

---

[10] Our organizational and networked motivations are similar to Bennett and Segerberg's (2012) distinction between "organization-based" and "self-organizing" mobilizations. Those authors further distinguish organizationally enabled (organizations in the background) from organizationally brokered (organizations play a leading role) mobilization. Another tradition, going back to Snow et al. (1986), uses the term "micromobilization" to refer to recruitment via individuals' personal networks. And of course, there is substantial work on the mobilizational power of networks when it comes to voter behavior (e.g., Bond et al. 2012; Nickerson 2008; Sinclair 2012).

(Wood 2003) or solidarity of identifying with a larger collective (Passy 2001). Pre-existing informal networks can serve as the backbone along which new movements and rebellions form (Shesterinina 2021; Staniland 2014; Tilly 1978; Tilly and Wood 2020) or which existing movements fall back on when repressed and driven underground (Parkinson 2022). How these networks work is thus a core question of social movements research.

We focus specifically on three key dimensions of interpersonal connections that have been widely studied in other movements but not with regard to the 2020 BLM protests. As explained in Section 1, these protests enveloped a movement in support of a marginalized group, with the use of social media, with a largely leaderless organization, and a concern for intersectionality. Insofar as these characteristics may well define many future movements, much can be gained by studying them, beyond enhancing what we know about one of the most impactful social movements in contemporary American times. The three dimensions of interpersonal relations we consider are (1) the strength of the relationship (tie strength), (2) whether each person is a movement insider or outsider, and (3) whether the tie connects a Black person to a non-Black person (cross-cleavage).

2.2 Tie Strength, Personal Recruitment, and Exposure

A long-standing debate in the mobilization literature focuses on the relative importance of strong versus weak ties. Given the ambiguity in usage, it is important that we offer a clear definition: for us, tie strength refers to the emotional closeness of the people a particular tie connects. Strong ties entail more closeness than weak ties, all else constant. Other concepts, such as triadic closure (e.g., sharing mutual friends) or communication frequency, may be correlated but are distinct from tie strength as we define it. For example, one can feel emotional closeness (i.e., a strong tie) without having common connections or speaking often (Brashears and Quintane 2018).

Strong ties have the advantage of stimulating attention and facilitating targeted messages. In terms of attention, people tend to focus on information that they believe will help them avoid mistakes (Lupia and McCubbins 1998). Close relationships presumably grow out of interactions that lead to more positive than negative outcomes. Thus, people attend more to those with whom they have strong ties. Strong ties also suggest knowledge about another's tastes, values, and interests. This allows one to craft targeted communications that resonate and can often be relatively persuasive (e.g., Hillygus and Shields 2009; Teeny et al. 2021).

This makes strong ties amenable to *personal recruitment* – that is, a one-on-one appeal to a potential recruit to attend a protest. Examples include a text message, phone call, or face-to-face conversation between a recruiter and the potential recruit. Personal recruitment can lead to (collective) action via persuasion with directed messages about the efficacy of the protest or the personal benefits of attending (e.g., making a difference, having fun, minimizing regret), detailed information about a protest, and/or offers to accompany the other to the protest, which leverages social pressure and provides social utility (i.e., satisfy interpersonal needs) (Walgrave and Ketelaars 2019). We previously distinguished frequency of communication from strong ties; however, all else constant, the more frequent those interactions with strong ties, the more successful personal recruitment might be (Centola 2018). This holds in part because frequency ensures familiarity with another's perspectives on the contemporary issues necessary for targeted messages (Roberts and Dunbar 2011).

While weak ties lack these attentional and targeting advantages, they compensate by facilitating access to large numbers of people and, in so doing, potentially invoking normative behaviors. Although, in general, people communicate directly more often with their strong ties (and may share more information when they do so), there are simply a lot more weak ties from which to get information in the first place. Most people have far more acquaintances than they do close friends (Lubbers, Molina, and Valenzuela-García 2019). From this perspective, the strength of weak ties is a strength in numbers.

Classic research on the subject (Granovetter 1973) suggests that our weaker social connections may provide useful nonredundant information not easily obtained in our closer social circles (see also Rajkumar et al. 2022). More recent empirical tests examining the utility of weak ties in a similar context note that, all else equal, a single strong tie provides more advantages, but weak ties tend to be numerous enough to more than compensate for their lower utility in the aggregate (Gee, Jones, and Burke 2017). An implication here is that while strong ties may play an important role in recruitment at the micro level, it is weak ties that knit together those micro contexts into a broader national movement.

More distant relationships mean targeted messages that receive substantial attention are unlikely. But the volume of messages – particularly when consistent – that one receives from their many weak ties makes *exposure* a relevant mechanism/strategy. Examples of exposure include seeing posts on social media (either public or directed to all of a user's friends/followers), watching the news, witnessing a protest, or receiving a mass text or email.[11] Exposure can play an essential coordinating role by providing brief information about time and place. It also can persuade via norms – in particular, descriptive norms where people learn that many others (via weak ties) are acting and thus

---

[11] We treat any one-to-one interaction as constituting at least a weak tie (i.e., we do not incorporate the possibility of a connection that is a non-tie).

feel as though they should act (e.g., Bayes et al. 2020; Fishbein and Ajzen 2009). The chorus of appeals to protest, announcements of the speaker's own intent to protest, and photos of them doing so may be especially effective at creating the impression that protesting is a desirable behavior – one that others would do well to adopt if they hope to fit in or enhance their social status.[12]

The potential to mobilize protesters through exposure via weak ties has dramatically increased since the advent of social media. Potential recruits may be exposed to the opinions and behavior of hundreds if not thousands of their weak ties on a weekly or daily basis. Most social media platforms are calibrated to show users content with which they are likely to interact ("like," retweet, click on, etc.). Tie strength will likely be correlated with content ranking, but many other factors influence a user's likelihood of reading or sharing a post, including its global popularity on the platform. Thus, there are likely to be enough posts prioritized for reasons other than inferred tie strength that users will end up seeing a lot more content from weak ties than from strong ones (Shmargad and Klar 2020). This could level the playing field for exposure through strong and weak ties. While a single strong tie may outweigh a single weak one in online visibility and persuasiveness, the balance shifts when we examine ties in the aggregate. Consider a person with one close friend and a hundred acquaintances. Social media substantially increases the likelihood that an individual will receive content – possibly more content – from acquaintances relative to a situation without social media.[13] We thus suspect that the effectiveness of social media at mobilizing protesters will not systematically depend on tie strength and, in particular, will not be contingent on strong ties. While personalized recruitment via strong ties can occur through social media, so can normative influence through many weakly tied social media messages.[14] So strong ties are not necessary per se.

Our discussion of the strength of ties and mobilization strategy leads to our first hypothesis, as follows:

---

[12] In addition to setting expectations for normative behavior, exposure can also reinforce a collective identity that can be important to political mobilization.

[13] The role of exposure for social movement mobilization has been neglected or downplayed even while an entirely separate literature focused on the online platforms has sprung up around it (e.g., Jackson, Bailey, and Welles 2020; Larson et al. 2019).

[14] This argument coheres with classic research on political mobilization (Klandermans 1984) that emphasizes the cost-benefit calculus underlying protest decisions. Social media can alter the perception of costs and benefits, regardless of tie strength, for example, by signaling levels of support via interactive features (e.g., "likes" or hashtags like #BlackLivesMatter). Additionally, the strength in weak ties underlying Hypothesis 1 may reflect a strength-in-numbers dynamic (Centola 2018, 201) or the bridging of disparate social circles (Granovetter 1973).

Hypothesis 1. Strong and weak ties are associated with different mobilization mechanisms. In particular:

a) Mobilization via personal recruitment will depend on strong ties more than weak ties.

b) Mobilization through social media exposure will not depend on strong ties.

In addition to this hypothesis, we expect differences between social media platforms in terms of their relevance to mobilization through strong versus weak ties. Specifically, Facebook's "friendship" ties must be mutual and consensual (Vitak, Ellison, and Steinfield 2011). Further, Facebook appears to use an algorithm that takes inferred tie strength (e.g., designated close friends, frequent contacts) into account in its content ranking.[15] This means there will be relatively less exposure to strangers and more exposure to close friends (strong ties) compared to other platforms such as Twitter, Instagram, and TikTok (Bucher 2012; Burke and Kraut 2014; Woo-Yoo and Gil-de-Zúñiga 2014).[16]

2.3 Mobilizing Movement Insiders versus Outsiders

Research on collective action and protest recruitment has long emphasized the importance of personal connections to highly engaged people who are already part of the movement (McAdam 1986; Walgrave, Wouters, and Ketelaars 2022). Social ties to activists, organizers, and participants in prior protest(s) – whom we collectively refer to as "insiders" – can provide relevant information, affect the perception of key social norms, and create a positive view of an activist identity (Passy 2001). This focus on the process of recruiting new participants (i.e., "outsiders") by insiders, however, leaves out an important part of the mobilization puzzle: What sorts of ties might "re-mobilize" insiders? And how does the mobilization of outsiders differ from that of insiders?[17]

We argue that insiders are mobilized through different channels relative to outsiders, due to the networks they are embedded in. Insiders are more likely to have pre-existing ties to other protest veterans and activists. They may be members

---

[15] The company announced in 2018 that it would aim to prioritize posts by friends and family, giving its users "more opportunities to interact with the people they care about." See https://about.fb.com/news/2018/01/news-feed-fyi-bringing-people-closer-together. Note that in addition to friendship, Facebook has a nonmutual "follow" option, but users must opt in to allow this.

[16] Along these lines, Valenzuela, Correa, and de Zúñiga (2018) report that Facebook is composed of stronger ties than Twitter.

[17] Our use of the terms "insiders" and "outsiders" largely aligns with others' terminology. Examples include McCarthy and Zald's (1977) "constituents" who provide resources to an organization (including time and labor) versus "adherents" who endorse a movement's goals (distinct from, for example, bystanders or opponents) and Klandermans' (2004, 2015) steps of how outsiders become mobilized into participants (e.g., having potential, being targeted, being motivated, overcoming barriers).

of social movement organizations or have signed up for an organizer's email list. They may be members of a social-justice-related Facebook or WhatsApp group or followers of a related Twitter or Instagram account. They may also have befriended other insiders at previous protests or even met their romantic partner through the movement. We thus expect insiders to have ample opportunity to be remobilized by other insiders. Consistent with McAdam's discussion of "costs" and "risks" (McAdam 1986; Wiltfang and McAdam 1991), we argue that people who are internal to the movement can use their pre-existing network ties as mobilizing resources to offset some of the challenge of protesting (cf. Tindall 2002, 2015). Conversely, outsiders will have fewer opportunities to be mobilized by insiders (Steinert-Threlkeld 2017).

Moreover, the social pressure that comes from having multiple members of one's network involved in a movement may be instrumental in pushing weary activists to return to the streets (see Gould 2003; Tufekci 2014). For an insider who is deeply embedded in activist circles, failure to remain involved in a movement may result in the loss of one's friends. This type of public exposure can be extremely impactful (Gerber, Green, and Larimer 2008; but see Gould 2003). Even insiders whose social life does not revolve around the movement may be motivated to protest by pressure from insider friends and the possibility of public expressions of disapproval on social media.[18] In addition to social pressure, insiders may be motivated by social utility – that is, the opportunity to socialize with their insider friends and acquaintances or the joy of taking part in a collective endeavor.

In contrast, most outsiders lack these socially based incentives. Rather than being embedded in an insider household or insider friend group, they are more likely to have a single link (if any) to activist circles. Even if an outsider knows multiple insiders, it is likely that these links serve as "bridges" between distinct circles of friends (Snow et al. 1986).[19] This does not preclude the ties from being strong – an outsider's best friend may be an activist – but it is unlikely that this outsider is an integral part of an activist friend group without having ever attended a protest. Thus, peer pressure from social media, the social utility of seeing friends, and intra-household ties should be less likely to motivate outsiders.

Since insiders have already experienced protesting and support the cause, seeing a Facebook post about a protest's time and place may be sufficient to get them to attend. Outsiders, in contrast, may need to be convinced of a movement's righteousness and the efficacy of protesting. Such persuasion could take place through personal recruitment in a one-on-one conversation (in person or online)

---

[18] This type of social pressure may be especially acute within a household, where one is very likely to know the activities of those with whom they live.

[19] In other contexts, a "bridge" could also refer to a tie between different racial groups or parts of an industry (Burt 2004).

or through exposure to moral shocks – for instance, the video of George Floyd's murder. In the case of BLM, since outsiders are less likely to be familiar with the issues involved and stories of victimization, hearing about the murder of an unarmed Black person might cause them to experience a greater moral shock (Jasper and Poulsen 1995). In fact, Alicia Garza's 2013 Facebook post about the acquittal of George Zimmerman for killing Trayvon Martin – the very post that popularized the phrase "Black Lives Matter" – was aimed, in part, at fellow insiders who she felt were no longer shocked by such verdicts: "btw stop saying we are not surprised. That's a damn shame in itself. I continue to be surprised at how little Black lives matter" (Cobb 2016). Thus, news and conscience may be stronger motivators for movement outsiders than insiders.

Another source of moral shock could come from knowing someone who was themselves a victim of the cause being protested – in this case, racism or police violence. A sizable literature shows that relaying personal experiences can persuade people to be more supportive of marginalized groups (e.g., Broockman and Kalla 2016; Kalla and Broockman 2020, 2023). This is particularly effective when an experience of harm or suffering is invoked (Kubin et al. 2021) – it "transports" the receiver into the story so that the receiver becomes focused on the world it depicts (Green and Brock 2000). In this case, it will pull upon individuals' perceptions of harm to others as well as their conscience, or their beliefs about what is "right." An implication is that by sharing their stories of discrimination and police brutality, Black people succeed in mobilizing those outside of their immediate social circles. An implicit part of the argument is that in this scenario, outsiders are swayed by persuasive messages via personal recruitment (e.g., learning of victimization) rather than by learning about social utility prospects, which might matter more to insiders.

Finally, hearing a friend who never talks about racism speak out for the first time may shock an outsider out of their complacency. Likewise, learning that a relative who has never gone to a protest feels moved to attend may signal important normative cues of the protest's import (Lohmann 1994). Thus, while insiders may be more likely to talk about racism or post pictures of themselves at protests, outsiders who engage in these forms of mobilization may have a stronger impact, per capita, on other first-time protesters.

We sum up these factors as follows:

Hypothesis 2: Movement insiders and outsiders will be mobilized through different channels as a result of the networks in which they are embedded.

- *Compared to outsiders, insiders are more likely to be:*
  - *Mobilized by other insiders,*
  - *Mobilized via social media exposure,*

  – *Mobilized via intra-household ties, and*
  – *Mobilized through appeals to social utility*

• *Compared to insiders, outsiders are more likely to be:*
  – *Mobilized via personal recruitment,*
  – *Mobilized via inter-household ties, and*
  – *Mobilized through moral shocks*

We expect this hypothesis to be especially relevant to summer 2020 protests, due to the costs, risks, and opportunities associated with BLM and the COVID-19 pandemic. First, protesting often involved the risk of clashes with police and violating social distancing guidelines at a time when vaccines were not yet available. Thus, moral shocks and personal recruitment may have been particularly essential in getting protesters to accept these elevated risks, particularly for outsiders who had never before protested. Second, the social isolation created by the pandemic may have made the opportunity to see friends at a protest an even more compelling motivation, particularly for insiders whose friends were more likely to be there. Third, the pandemic led Americans to spend more time on the internet and social media.[20] Insiders may thus have been more likely to see posts announcing protests – and get the impression that "everyone" in their social world was showing up – than if they had spent less time on their devices. Outsiders, likewise, may have had more exposure to moral shocks (e.g., viral videos, news, posts from victims). The impact on personal recruitment, however, was probably mixed – more messages through apps but fewer face-to-face conversations.

Our hypothesis differs from older work on networks and social movements, which often portrays insiders as the driving force in recruiting new movement members (see Gould 2003). For instance, a central finding of McAdam's *Freedom Summer* is that links to people already involved in the civil rights struggle proved crucial in persuading college students to volunteer (McAdam 1988).[21] Summing up research prior to the advent of social media, Schussman and Soule write, "The presence of a network tie to someone already engaged in a movement is one of the strongest predictors of individual participation in the movement" (2005, 1068). We agree with this assessment, but we add the caveat that it is fellow insiders – not new participants – who are most likely to be mobilized in this way. In contrast, it is victims (regardless of their insider/outsider status) who are best positioned to reach outsiders in a movement such

---

[20] As seen, for instance, in statistics reported by the Pew Research Center: www.pewresearch.org/internet/2021/09/01/the-internet-and-the-pandemic/.

[21] However, it is worth considering that these White students from elite Northern colleges were unlikely to have existing ties to the people they sought to empower: low-income, rural Black people in Mississippi.

as BLM. Our distinct prediction reflects both the movement's focus on the plight of a marginalized group and the evolving social structure of American society, to which we now turn.

2.4 Interracial Contact and Cross-Cleavage Capital

Cleavages between groups fundamentally define political systems (Lipset and Rokkan 1967). For hundreds of years, race has divided the United States, particularly along the lines of Black versus non-Black Americans (e.g., Alesina, Glaeser, and Sacerdote 2001). This manifests in sizable racial gaps in areas such as medical care (Ryn and Burke 2000), employment (Quillian et al. 2017), and political responsiveness (Costa 2017). White Americans also move in a conservative direction when presented with the threat of demographic changes toward diversity that might undermine their status (Craig and Richeson 2014). Certain disparities grew dramatically worse during COVID-19, with mortality among Black Americans being three to four times higher than that for White Americans (Andrasfay and Goldman 2021). Against that back-drop, a central aim of the BLM protests was not only to address the murder of George Floyd and other unarmed Black Americans but also to advocate for systemic change with regard to race.

Social scientists have long studied how interpersonal contact between an advantaged group and a marginalized group has the potential to diminish prejudice (e.g., Allport 1954). For instance, as contact with Black people increases, racial prejudice among White people decreases (see Pettigrew and Tropp [2006] and Paluck, Green, and Green [2019] for a review of the litera-ture). Contact can shape attitudes by counteracting stereotypes and allowing for the exchange of experiential narratives that tend to increase support for a marginalized group among members of an advantaged group (e.g., Kalla and Broockman 2020). We expect this to be particularly effective with regard to intentional intergroup contact – specifically, cross-racial contact, when a Black individual encourages actions by a non-Black individual. Along these lines, Hässler et al. (2020) show that intergroup contact increases support for low-cost collective actions (e.g., signing an online petition), high-cost collect-ive actions (e.g., demonstrating), empowering policies (e.g., ensuring the dis-advantaged group has more decision-making power), raising ingroup awareness, and working in solidarity. Hong and Peoples (2021) show that, in White individuals, relatively higher levels of intergroup contact with Black individuals correlate with a higher likelihood of participation in the BLM movement (not only through protest) prior to 2020. We expect the same dynamic to occur in the context of the 2020 BLM protests – non-Black individuals will be more likely to protest due to ties with Black individuals rather than due to ties with non-Black individuals. In the case of strong ties, we expect to see more impactful personal recruitment that accentuates personal experience, so Black recruiters should have a disproportionate influence. In the context of weak ties, hearing repeated pleas for help and learning of expressions of distress reinforce the impression that racism and police violence are systemic and widespread. Both mobilization mechanisms can be captured by non-Black protesters reporting that a major motivation for joining the movement was knowing someone who has been harmed by racism and/or police violence.

One way to conceptualize the importance of intergroup contact is via a particular type of social capital: *cross-cleavage capital* (Simonson 2021). While definitions of social capital are manifold (e.g., Adler and Kwon 2002; Coleman 1988; Lin 1999), we define it as the ability to get other people to help you. Social capital depends on the size of one's social network, the strength of one's ties, the willingness of those in one's network to help out, and the skills and resources they have to offer. This definition extends to the community level: a community with high social capital is one in which people can readily get help from one another, due perhaps to norms of reciprocity, dense social networks of strong ties, community members' connections to well-resourced outsiders (which they are willing to share), or some combination thereof (Coleman 1988; Putnam 2000).

Putnam (2000) talks about the "bridging" aspect of social capital as the extent to which assistance extends across discrete communities or social circles, often connecting people from different backgrounds. This is a useful starting place, but to understand BLM, we need to distinguish ties that form bridges between insiders and outsiders and ties that form bridges between Black people and non-Black people. We, therefore, define *cross-cleavage capital* as one's ability to muster assistance across a major society-wide social or political cleavage such as race in the United States (Simonson 2021).[22] An individual or a community may be high in social capital in general, but if that individual lacks ties to other races or the community's social network is deeply segregated, then they are lacking in cross-cleavage capital. A lack of cross-cleavage capital can reinforce social inequalities, such as when members of a marginalized group lack the connections needed to get a job, find a good

---

[22] This has some similarity to Blau and Schwartz's (1997) concept of cross-cutting social circles (based initially on Georg Simmel's work) where social structure consists of overlapping social circles that generate a web of individual group affiliations. Our focus is on how one can obtain assistance from those in one circle when they reside in another, perhaps due partially to overlap in a shared other circle (e.g., social contact, geography) (also see Blau 1993).

doctor or lawyer, or get their children into a good school (Massey and Denton 2019). For the both disadvantaged and the advantaged group, cross-cleavage capital facilitates cultural competency thanks to interpersonal contact with members of the disadvantaged group. Cross-cleavage capital is important for minority protest because it makes abstract injustices concrete via contact. Would-be protesters may see protest not only as a response to a past injustice but as a means of preventing future injustices from happening to those they know – those who have countered stereotypes and provided portraits of victimhood. Protest, then, can be seen as a form of helping.

This idea extends to the community level. We expect non-Black people who live in areas with more Black people will have a higher likelihood of cross-racial interactions due to higher cross-cleavage capital in their communities. Brown et al. (2021) use data that include the residential context of virtually all Americans in 1940; they then look at how that context subsequently affected the political behavior of men alive seventy years later. They find that early-life exposure to Black neighbors predicts Democratic partisanship of White men more than seventy years later. This echoes the aforementioned work on interpersonal contact where intergroup exposure liberalizes the political attitudes of White people (e.g., Green and Wong 2009). Because they are more integrated and thus contain multiracial networks, these are examples of communities with high cross-cleavage capital shaping the political attitudes of advantaged group members. We expect a similar dynamic with protests. By protesting, the advantaged group member helps the entire "imagined community" of the disadvantaged (Anderson 1983), but, more importantly, they are helping flesh-and-blood people whom they know and care about. Thus, we expect communities with higher cross-cleavage capital – where majority group members are used to helping minority individuals and where minority group members can readily call on majority group members for assistance – to exhibit more majority group protest. In short, non-Black individuals will be more likely to protest as the geographic area in which they live becomes more racially diverse, all else constant.

Hypothesis 3: As cross-cleavage capital increases, so will the likelihood of protesting. This is captured by:

(a) *Non-Black individuals will be more likely to protest due to ties with Black individuals (than due to ties with non-Black individuals).*
(b) *Non-Black individuals from more diverse communities will be more likely to protest (relative to those from less diverse communities).*

(Note that while there are multiple racial cleavages in America, as well as nonracial cleavages such as party, in this Element we will use "cleavage" to refer to Black–non-Black relations.)

Hypothesis 3 speaks to the importance of social penumbras – the set of outgroup members who know someone in a particular group (Gelman and Margalit 2021). The prediction suggests that non-Black protesters are drawn disproportionately from the social penumbra of Black Americans – and, in all likelihood, the social penumbra of Black Americans willing to share their personal stories of discrimination and police violence. This could have occurred just after George Floyd's murder or before it (we discuss network selection effects when we analyze the data). While thousands of Americans have marched under banners reading "Save Darfur" or "Free Tibet" without knowing a single Darfuri or Tibetan, these movements never attracted mass participation by millions of Americans from across the political landscape seen in 2020.

2.5 Conclusion

The 2020 BLM protests were unprecedented. The majority of protesters were non-Black individuals, participating in protests aimed – at least in part – at combating violence and racism against Black people. Moreover, the protests took place in the context of a movement that leveraged social media and had a decentralized structure. This intersection of factors leads us to offer a novel set of hypotheses of how mobilization worked in 2020. We predict that the primary drivers of these protests were (1) weak ties (and strangers) exposing people to motivating content on social media, (2) the mobilization of outsiders through personal recruitment and moral shocks, and (3) the mobilization of non-Black allies through cross-cleavage ties. If this is the case, it would showcase how twenty-first-century American social movements can spring into action with mobilization tactics that historically have proven less central. Strong emotional connections matter less, organizational insiders matter less, and within-cleavage connections matter less. It would signify a new era of protest mobilization – or, at least, a widening of what sorts of mobilization are now possible.[23]

We next turn to describing our data in Section 3, and then testing our hypotheses in Sections 4, 5, and 6. To facilitate reading, we provide key terminology and definitions (as discussed throughout Section 2) in Table 1 and a summary of our hypotheses in Table 2.

---

[23] More generally, the diffusion of ideas and behavioral contagion often require social reinforcement (Centola 2010). Our theory suggests that this need not depend on strong ties since the volume and visibility of messages via weak ties can reveal the wide acceptance of ideas. Further, our theory suggests a way to overcome homophily through cross-cleavage connections.

Table 1 Key terms and definitions

Term	Definition
Tie	Any type of social relationship
Alter	A person to whom one is connected by a tie (e.g., friend, relative, neighbor, etc.)
Tie strength	The emotional strength of a relationship. A close friend or family member would be considered a strong tie; an acquaintance, a weak tie
Personal recruitment	A personalized one-on-one appeal to join a protest via a message or conversation (online or face to face)
Social media exposure	Exposure to norms, peer pressure, or information about a protest through posts on social media. May be public or limited to one's friends/followers, but is not an individualized one-on-one appeal
Insiders	Individuals with prior involvement in a given movement, including membership in an organization or prior attendance at protests
Outsiders	Individuals who have never protested (for any cause)
Cross-cleavage capital	Capacity to summon assistance or support from people on the other side of a social cleavage (e.g., a racial divide)
Cross-cleavage tie	A tie that spans a social cleavage (in this case, connecting a Black person to a non-Black person)

3 Measuring Mobilization

3.1 The COVID States Project

Our data come from the COVID States Project (www.covidstates.org), a nationwide longitudinal survey with a quota-based sample of US adults. Respondents are recruited through a digital platform that uses multiple online survey panel vendors. Part of the sample is retained across multiple surveys. Depending on the vendor, panelists are either volunteers or are rewarded with points that can be redeemed for cash or other incentives. The data collection was reviewed and approved by the Northeastern University Institutional Review Board (#20–04–12).

After deduplicating and filtering out problematic respondents, we reweighted our sample to match the US adult population on interlocked race-gender-age subgroups as well as education, rurality, and region, based on the 2019 American Community Survey from the US Census Bureau.[24] From this pool of respondents,

---

[24] We employ these weights whenever we report percentages.

Table 2 Summary of hypotheses

Hyp.	Key variable	Prediction (a)	Prediction (b)
1	Tie strength between mobilizer and target (strong/weak)	Mobilization via personal recruitment will depend on strong ties more than weak ties.	Mobilization through social media exposure will not depend on strong ties.
2	Target's prior involvement (insider/outsider)	Compared to outsiders, insiders are more likely to be mobilized by other insiders, social media exposure, intra-household ties, and appeals to social utility.	Compared to insiders, outsiders are more likely to be mobilized via personal recruitment, interhousehold ties, and moral shocks.
3	Mobilizer's race (Black/Non-Black)	Non-Black individuals will be more likely to protest due to ties with Black individuals (than due to ties with non-Black individuals).	Non-Black individuals from more diverse communities will be more likely to protest (relative to those from less diverse communities).

we obtain similar estimates for key political and public health outcomes to traditional probability-based surveys from Gallup, Ipsos, and Pew Research, as shown in Green et al. (2023). In addition, estimates of COVID-19 vaccination rates by state derived from our (weighted) sample are strongly correlated with, and sometimes clearly superior to, official statistics (Lazer 2022; Lazer et al. 2023).[25]

For this study, we examine nine survey waves conducted between June 12, 2020, and December 1, 2020, with a total of 141,188 observations of 101,017 unique respondents. We refer to this as our **main dataset.** Of these respondents, 5,449 said they attended a "rally, vigil or protest" about "racism and/or police violence" in the month leading up to the survey. Respondents were not told the topic of the survey before entering, and the vast majority of the questionnaire before the protest module focused on public health, the election, and economic

---

[25] On using statistical significance tests with nonprobability samples (that identify population attributes that correlate with key statistics and balance/weight the sample on those attributes, as in our case), see Groves et al. (2009, 409–10), and Vehovar, Toepoel, and Steinmetz (2016, 342).

topics. Thus, while there may be unobserved differences between respondents and the US public that weighting does not account for, the risk of selection bias based on the topic itself is minimized. Our overall rate of protest participation in June 2020 (4.5 percent) falls within the confidence intervals of the Pew (Parker, Horowitz, and Anderson 2020) and AP-NORC surveys from that time.[26] We also draw on data from two subsequent survey waves, which we refer to as the **December retrospective wave** and the **summer 2022 retrospective wave**, respectively. The December retrospective wave ($N = 20,344$), which ran from December 16, 2020, to January 11, 2021, asked respondents about any Black Lives Matter protests they attended in 2020, rather than merely in the past month. In response to this version of the question, 4.9 percent of respondents reported having protested. We do not use these data in our primary analysis, since protesters are less likely to remember motivations months later, but we do use them as a robustness check in the Online Appendix. Subsequent waves of the COVID States Survey did not ask about protests until 2022. The summer 2022 retrospective wave ($N = 20,098$), which ran June 8–July 8, 2022, asked about protest attendance since the start of the pandemic.[27] It also included two sets of questions about cross-racial social ties, discussed in Sections 3.4.2 and 3.4.4.

3.2 Protest Motivations

The sheer size of our sample enables us to measure not only which types of individuals were likely to protest but also what the protesters themselves have to say about the recruitment process. From June to November 2020 (i.e., all waves in the main dataset), respondents who said they had attended a protest were presented with a list of motivations in the order shown and asked to check all that applied (variable names are in parentheses):

(1) People I knew were posting about it on social media (*social media*)
(2) Reading or watching the news (*news*)
(3) Someone encouraged me, personally, to attend in a message or conversation (*conversation*)
(4) One of the event organizers contacted me (*organizer*)
(5) My conscience (*conscience*)
(6) Faith or religious values (*faith*)
(7) Wanted to see people I know in person (*see alters*)
(8) Wanted a reason to leave the house (*leave house*)

---

[26] AP-NORC summary: https://apnorc.org/wp-content/uploads/2020/06/Topline_final_release5.pdf.

[27] These very large samples provide the rare opportunity to use surveys to study hard-to-reach populations (see Bayes, Druckman, and Safarpour 2022).

(9) It sounded interesting, fun, or exciting (*fun*)

(10) An organization or a group I belong to was directly involved (*membership*)

(11) Because I have been harmed by racism and/or police violence (*harm to self*)

(12) Because someone I know was harmed by racism and/or police violence (*harm to alter*)

In Section 2.1, we distinguished personal motivations, organizational motivations, and social network motivations to protest while suggesting social networks would be most prominent in this case. In Figure 1, we straightforwardly characterize each motive into one of these categories. While respondents were free to select multiple options, relatively few (21 percent) chose an organizational motivation, whereas 81 percent selected at least one social networked motivation and 83 percent chose a personal motivation. That personal motivations match socially networked motivations is not something we necessarily expected; however, more important for us is that socially networked motivations far exceed organizational ones. Of course, self-reported motivations are never free from bias. Respondents may, for instance, omit *see alters* as a reason for fear of being seen as opportunistic or insincere. They may omit *conversation* because they forgot about a conversation they had with a friend. And they may omit *social media* because, though they recall using it, they do not realize that it motivated them. On the other hand, people are unlikely to forget that they were members of an organization.[28] Thus, the gap between organizational motivations and socially networked motivations may be even wider than our data suggest. Regardless, as expected, socially networked motivations dwarfed organizational ones.[29]

We will return to these data for (partial) tests of our hypotheses (e.g., Hypothesis 1 regarding the role of social media). In so doing, it is important to clarify that what we term socially networked mobilization here in Figure 1 is not necessarily related to whether mobilization is done by those tied to the organization or not (as discussed in Section 2). We turn to this distinction in Section 5.

---

[28] Though they may forget that they were contacted by an organizer. Interestingly, respondents with a higher income or education are more likely to report organizational motivations, particularly *organizer*.

[29] As stated, there are long-standing concerns about asking for self-reported motivations, because individuals may lack the introspective ability to explicate rationales, and, as mentioned, there could be a tendency to misreport, such as overreporting what they view as more admirable motivations (e.g., Fulmer and Frijters 2009). That said, we follow others who study motivations for protests by relying on self-reports (e.g., Tropp and Uluğ 2019; Walgrave and Wourters 2014). We address common concerns by allowing multiple responses. Further, our results make clear respondents did not only report socially desirable options, with more than half reporting attending a protest because they saw people they knew posting about it on social media (somewhat of a conformity dynamic).

Motivation for attending protests

Percentage of respondents who selected each motivation for protest attendance.
Black points are percent estimates, with 95 percent confidence intervals in gray.

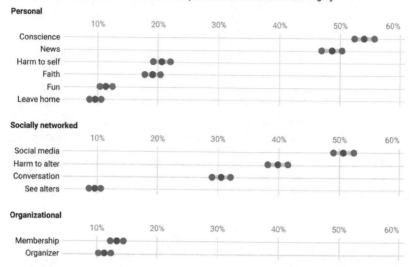

Figure 1 Percentage of protesters who cite each motivation for attending
a protest. Estimates are weighted to census benchmarks

3.3 Insiders and Outsiders

To test Hypothesis 2 about movement insiders and outsiders, we asked respondents if they had "been to other rallies, protests or vigils prior to the past month." The response options were:

a. Yes, for this cause
b. Yes, for a different cause
c. No, this was my first
d. I don't remember

Given the unprecedented turnout at protests in the weeks after the murder of George Floyd, it is perhaps not surprising that only 35 percent of protesters in the June 2020 wave said they had attended a protest "for this cause" prior to the last month. Nearly half (44 percent) had never attended a protest before, while 18 percent had attended a protest for "a different cause" and 4 percent couldn't remember. We coded respondents who answered (a) as *insiders* and those who answered (c) as *outsiders*. The status of those who answered (b) is ambiguous, however, since they may include respondents for whom both (a) and (b) are applicable as well as respondents for which only (b) applies. Therefore, we chose to focus our insider-outsider analyses (Hypothesis 2) on unambiguous insiders (a) and unambiguous outsiders (c).

3.4 Capturing Ties

Table 3 provides an overview of the tie-related variables we measured. The attributes column often indicates follow-up questions, such as whether the tie was strong or weak or if the other person was Black.

3.4.1 Protest-Specific Ties

The following sets of questions were included in all waves up through the December 2020 retrospective wave.

Recruiters: Respondents who selected the *conversation* item from the list of motivations (see section 3.2) were then asked, "Who encouraged you, personally, to attend? (Please select all that apply)," with the following options:

a. Someone in my household
b. Someone outside my household I'm close with
c. Someone outside my household I'm not so close with
d. Someone I've never met in person

We refer to this alter as a *recruiter*. We classify the tie between respondent and *recruiter* as *strong* if they chose (a) or (b), *weak* if they chose (c), and *stranger* if they chose (d). These responses allow us to test the part of Hypothesis 1 concerning the association between strong ties and personal recruitment.

Companions: All protesters were asked if they attended with anyone else and their relationship to that *companion*, which we classified as *strong* (both household and non-household), *weak* (non-household), or none. Like the *recruiter* questions, these questions are used to test Hypotheses 1 (tie strength) and 2 (insider/outsider ties).

Mobilizers: All protesters, regardless of whether they chose the *conversation* item, were then asked a series of questions about the person who had the biggest influence on their decision to attend, referred to here as the *mobilizer*. Specifically, they were asked whether their *mobilizer* was someone they had a close relationship with (used to test H1), a self-described activist, a person who had already attended protests for this cause (i.e., an insider – used to test H2), and/or Black (used to test H3). We also asked if they lived within an hour's drive, were a relative under age thirty, or had encouraged the respondent to protest via social media.

Recruitment Efforts: All protesters were later asked whether they had attempted to persuade anyone else to protest (*recruitment attempt*) and,

Table 3 Variables and definitions

Variable	Definition	Attributes
Recruiter	Alter who encouraged the respondent to protest through a message or conversation	Strong (household or non-household), weak, stranger
Companion	Alter who accompanied the respondent to a protest	Strong (household or non-household), weak, none
Mobilizer	Alter with biggest impact on the respondent's decision to protest	Activist, prior protester, close tie, Black, young relative, local, social media tie
Recruitment efforts	The respondent tried to recruit someone (regardless of outcome)	Attempt (regardless of outcome), success, overall impact
Strong non-household ties	Alters with 3 strongest relationships outside of the respondent's household	Attended protest, had COVID, race, etc.
Social support ties	Number of people the respondent can count on for various forms of support	Support ties average
Cross-racial tie strength	Whether the respondent had known any Black people (if non-Black) or non-Black people (if Black) for more than three years, and nature of relationship	Strong, friend, acquaintance
Sharing stories	Whether a Black respondent shared stories with others of racism, victimization. Whether a non-Black respondent had received such a story	Shared story (conversation), shared story (social media)
Encourage protest	Whether a Black respondent encourages non-Black people to attend a protest. Whether a non-Black respondent had received such encouragement	Encouraged protest (conversation), encouraged protest (social media)

Table 3 (cont.)

Variable	Definition	Attributes
Neighborhood ties	Percentage of residents in the respondent's ZIP Code who are Black	Black population share
Social media ties	Which social media platforms the respondent is a member of	TikTok, Snapchat, Facebook, etc.

among those who did, whether they had been successful (*recruitment success*). We calculate the *overall impact* as the proportion of protesters that both attempted and succeeded. These questions are brought to bear on all three hypotheses.

3.4.2 Strong Non-Household Ties

In addition to asking about social network ties involved in protest recruitment, we also ask about respondents' social networks in general. In the June 2020 survey wave, we asked respondents to list the "three people living outside your household with whom you have the strongest, closest relationship." We refer to these alters as *strong non-household ties*, and we analyze these data at the alter-respondent dyad level (i.e., one row for each tie), clustering standard errors on the respondent. Although we assume these ties are all strong, we include two variables that may be indicative of which of these ties are strongest. First, we include *alter order*, a variable that indicates whether a given alter was the first, second, or third alter the respondent listed (respondents were asked to write each alter's initials to be used in subsequent questions). Second, we asked respondents about the frequency of their communication with each alter before the pandemic (*habitual communication*). The original question had seven options, which we collapsed into three categories for ease of interpretation: daily (every day or multiple times per day), weekly (several times per week or once a week), and monthly (several times per month, once a month, or less than once a month).

We next asked about the frequency of communication with each alter in the past week (*recent communication*). This variable helps us to differentiate personal recruitment, which requires recent communication, from other mechanisms. The original question had five options that we collapsed into four: daily (every day or multiple times per day), several times, once, and none.

The *alter protest* variable records whether each alter had attended a protest in the past two weeks. Two caveats should be noted here. First, we did not specify the protest cause. That said, among respondents, BLM protests were five times more common than lockdown/reopening protests, so the vast majority of these protesting alters are probably BLM protesters. Second, respondents do not always know whether their alter protested. In our analyses, we drop all respondent-alter dyads where the respondent chose "not sure." However, for robustness, we also ran the same analyses by coding the "not sure" responses as "no" and found that it made little difference to our findings.

We included two additional alter characteristics with a potential link to protesting: *alter covid*, since having an alter with COVID-19 may increase one's sense of grievance, and *alter police*, since having a close tie to a police officer may make one less sympathetic to rallies calling to defund the police.[30] Finally, we also included how respondents and alters knew each other: *alter family*, *alter friend*, *alter neighbor*, *alter coworker*, and *alter classmate* (multiple options could be selected).

Since these questions are relatively time-consuming, they were shown to a random 45 percent of respondents in June 2020 ($N = 9,750$) and then dropped from subsequent waves. Later, when we began analyzing BLM protests, we saw the need for greater detail. Therefore, in the summer 2022 retrospective wave, we reintroduced this battery for all BLM protesters ($n = 714$), as well as a randomly chosen 11 percent of non-protesters ($n = 2,147$). In this wave, we asked the race of each alter (*alter black, alter white, etc.*) and replaced the COVID-19 and protest questions with the following battery:

> *To the best of your knowledge, which of the following things has happened to each person since the start of the COVID-19 pandemic (since March 1, 2020)? (Please select all that apply, leave empty if not sure):*
>
> *a. Got sick with COVID-19*
> *b. Got vaccinated at least once*
> *c. Attended a protest against racism or police violence*
> *d. Regularly wore a mask*

By mixing the protest item with unrelated behaviors, we sought to obscure our interest in protests to limit demand effects (i.e., respondents attempting to tell the researcher what they want to hear). Although ideally, we would have asked these questions in June 2020 when the protests were unfolding, we believe this retrospective question can still provide a useful, if noisy, signal adding nuance

---

[30] We asked about police amid a list of other first responder and frontline worker professions.

to our understanding of the influence of tie strength (Hypothesis 1) and cross-racial alters (Hypothesis 3) on protest behavior.

3.4.3 Social Support Ties

Respondents in every survey wave were asked how many people in their "complete social circle of family, friends, neighbors, and other acquaintances" they could rely on to lend them money, care for them if they got sick, talk to if they had a problem or felt sad, or help them find a job.[31] We averaged these four measures to create an index called *support ties average*. Response options ranged from 0 to "11 or more." The median number of each type of tie was 2, except for the "someone to talk to" ties, which had a median of 3. We consider all of these ties to be strong and therefore use them to test Hypothesis 1 about the relationship between tie strength and mobilization mechanisms.

3.4.4 Cross-Racial Ties

For the June 2022 retrospective wave, we also added a question probing whether the respondent had any cross-racial ties. Non-Black respondents, including all non-Black protesters ($n = 613$) and a random 20 percent of non-Black respondents who did not protest ($n = 3,361$), were asked "Are there any African American or Black people that you have known for more than three years?" All Black respondents ($n = 2,319$) were shown this version of the question: "Are there any people of a race different from yours that you have known for more than three years?" (In both versions, the response options were "yes," "no," and "not sure.") We then asked follow-up questions about these alters, which we discuss here.

Tie Strength: For those who said yes to having cross-racial ties for at least three years, we asked: "Were any of them . . ."

a. Longtime acquaintances (e.g., colleagues or neighbors with whom you are not close)
b. Longtime friends
c. Relatives

Since respondents were permitted to check multiple options, we created a *strongest tie* variable indicating the strongest type of cross-racial tie the respondent reported (on the assumption that relatives tend to be closer than friends which are closer than acquittances).

---

[31] In the June 2020 wave, these questions were randomly shown to only 35 percent of respondents. Beginning in July 2020, all respondents were shown this question, including in the two retrospective waves we analyze.

Sharing Stories: We then asked Black respondents if they had shared personal stories of racism or victimization with their longtime non-Black alters. Non-Black respondents were asked if a Black alter had shared such a story with them. Response options included:

a. Yes, in a personal message or conversation
b. Yes, by posting to social media
c. No
d. Don't remember

The variables *shared story* (*conversation*) and *shared story* (*social media*) indicate whether a respondent selected those options (respondents could select both).

Encourage Protest: Finally, we asked Black respondents if they had encouraged any of their non-Black alters to attend a protest against racism or police violence since the start of the pandemic. Non-Black respondents were asked if a Black alter had encouraged them. Response options were identical to those in the "sharing stories" question, and we coded the variables *encouraged protest (conversation)* and *encouraged protest (social media)* accordingly.

These questions allow us to further address both Hypothesis 1 (the role of tie strength) and Hypothesis 3 (the role of cross-racial ties). We also use them to investigate whether the learning of personal encounters with racism is an important pathway for driving non-Black turnout.

Our approach with these survey items is intended to complement the approach utilized in the "strong non-household ties" battery. In the latter, respondents were forced to pre-commit to three individuals by writing down their initials without knowing what we would ask about them. This reduces social desirability bias (i.e., naming cross-racial friends to present oneself as open-minded), but it limits our view to the three closest alters. The "cross-racial network" battery takes the opposite approach, risking social desirability effects in exchange for allowing us to ask about a respondent's entire social network and subsequently distinguish between strong and weak ties. Both approaches are imperfect, but together they can paint a more complete picture of the role cross-racial ties played in motivating non-Black turnout.

Neighborhood Ties: We examine the racial composition of a respondent's ZIP Code, as measured by the 2020 census (for Hypothesis 3b). The variable *Black pop share* records the proportion of residents living in a respondent's ZIP Code who self-identified as Black or African American on the 2020 census.[32] ZIP Code racial composition provides a fairly objective measure of exposure to members of the outgroup, automatically available for every respondent. However, it is also less precise. We do not know whether respondents were actually friendly with their neighbors or whether Black residents live exclusively in one part of the ZIP Code area and White residents in another. Nevertheless, together with our *strong non-household* and *cross-racial* batteries, as well as the question about whether the *mobilizer* was Black, we can piece together a fuller understanding of the impact of Black people's networks on the population at large.

3.4.5 Social Media Ties

We asked all respondents which, if any, social media platforms they use. Of the fourteen included in the survey, we focus on the eight most popular in our analysis: *Facebook, YouTube, Instagram, Twitter, Snapchat, TikTok, WhatsApp,* and *Reddit*. We group these platforms into three categories based on the strength of ties expected to predominate in each case. The first category, *messaging platforms*, consists of apps geared toward direct messaging: Snapchat and WhatsApp. Although users can, in theory, participate in group chats with people they barely know, we expect messaging more often takes place between users who know one another offline. At the very least, users tend to have direct mutual interactions over the app in a one-on-one or small-group setting.

The second category, *friending platforms*, consists solely of Facebook, a social media space that requires "friendships" to be mutual. The platform also limits how many ties a person can acquire. Here we expect to find more weak ties than among the *messaging platforms*, though the mutuality requirement helps impose a lower bound on how weak these ties can be. As with the *messaging platforms*, many of those friends are likely to be alters that the user already knew or had met offline before connecting on Facebook. However, the ability to post to all of one's friends simultaneously means the users could be receiving information related to protests from people with whom they have not had direct interactions in years.

The third category, *following platforms*, consists of platforms where ties ("followers") need not be mutual. By default, this one-way connection does not even require the permission of the person being followed.[33] There is also no limit

---

[32] Our location data come from respondents' self-reported ZIP Code. Since the census does not report statistics by ZIP Code, we used a census-tract-to-ZCTA (ZIP Code Tabulation Area) crosswalk table to infer the racial composition of a respondent's ZIP Code.

[33] These categories are meant to reflect how the platforms are primarily used, even if there are exceptions. For instance, Facebook friendships are mutual by default, but users can change their settings to allow non-friends to follow them. Conversely, Instagram accounts are public by default, but users can change their settings to make their content private or require approval for new followers. Likewise, Facebook users (in addition to interacting with friends) can post to groups or follow pages, Instagram and Twitter users (in addition to posting and following) can message other users, and so forth.

Social media platform use among protesters and all Americans

Percentage of users of each platform among protesters and the full sample of respondents.

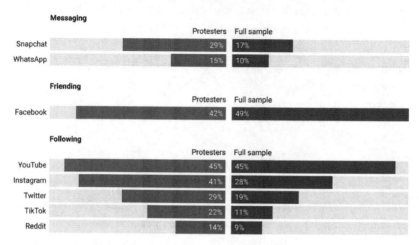

Figure 2 Popularity of social media platforms among the full sample and protesters. Estimates are weighted to census benchmarks

to the number of followers one can acquire. Platforms in this category include Instagram, Twitter, TikTok, Reddit, and YouTube. Here, in addition to friends and acquaintances, we expect to find the weakest ties of all – individuals who have no offline connection and have never directly communicated. Arguably, we might not consider these to be "ties" in a social network sense, even if they function as such in a communication network. Nonetheless, tie strength on those platforms remains a spectrum. Users who initially do not know each other but frequently interact in an online forum can develop a strong connection over time. Even so, most connections that we would classify as social ties on Twitter or Reddit tend to be weak. Thus, users of *following platforms* can be expected to receive a substantial portion of that platform's content through weak ties.

Figure 2 compares the percentage of protesters using each platform and to the percentage of all our respondents who use it. For every platform (except YouTube and Facebook), protesters are overrepresented compared to the rest of the population. This may be because younger Americans are more likely to use most of these platforms (except Facebook[34]) and are more likely to protest.[35]

---

[34] Compared to other platforms, Facebook users tend to be older (see www.pewresearch.org/internet/fact-sheet/social-media).

[35] Respondents in an online survey are, by definition, internet users and hence slightly more likely than the average American to be on social media. Since the missing (offline) population is likely older – and hence, less likely to protest – the gaps we observe in social media usage may in reality be even wider.

3.5 Measuring Race

Asking respondents about their race or ethnicity invariably involves trade-offs. For most of the duration of the COVID States Project, we relied on the race variable used by our recruitment company PureSpectrum to screen respondents for survey quotas. Originally, PureSpectrum's *race* question forced respondents to choose a single race from the following list: "White," "Hispanic," "African American," "Asian," "Middle Eastern," "American Indian," "Native Alaskan, Inuit or Aleut," "Native Hawaiian/Pacific Islander," "Other ethnicity," or "Prefer not to answer." Unfortunately, this format prevented respondents from selecting multiple races. Moreover, in contrast to the US Census, "Hispanic" was included in this list rather than being asked about separately.[36] In the summer 2022 retrospective survey wave, we chose to ask our own race question, which allowed respondents to choose multiple options (including Hispanic). Our weighting scheme for summer 2022 is still based on PureSpectrum's race question (for simplicity), but for analyses, we use the choose-all-that-apply version. Respondents who did not select any race (nor select "other") were dropped from the sample.

3.6 Controls

In addition to race, demographic control variables include *male*,[37] *age*, *generation*,[38] *income*,[39] *education* (no college, some college, four-year degree, graduate degree), *student* (dichotomous)*, religiosity* (frequency of attendance at religious services), and *party* (Democrat, Republican, independent, other), we also include variables that we believe are likely to affect a respondent's availability and communication networks: *household size* and whether the respondent was a *parent*, had a *significant other*, or had a job that required them to *work outside home* (despite the pandemic). Relatedly, the variable *disruptions* counts the

---

[36] Many Hispanic Americans do not consider Hispanic to be a racial category and some prefer other terms like Latino/a/x.

[37] Anyone who is not female. As with the race question, we relied on PureSpectrum's gender screening question for all waves, except the summer 2022 retrospective wave, in which we used our own. PureSpectrum's version offered only male or female, while our version allowed for other options.

[38] Although generational cutoffs are arbitrary, we chose to divide the *age* variable into categories to account for nonlinearities. For instance, protest participation or social media usage might drop steeply in the late twenties and then remain flat or decrease gradually. Following the Pew Research Center (https://pewrsr.ch/2szqtJz), we split age into four generations: Gen Z (ages 18–23 in 2020), Millennial (24–39), Gen X (40–55), and Boomer+ (56+). The "Boomer+" category combines the Baby Boomer generation with respondents older than seventy-four because the latter contains few protesters in our sample.

[39] Following the Pew Research Center (www.pewresearch.org/social-trends/2022/04/20/method ology-49/), *income* is adjusted for household size and split into three categories: high (at least twice the national median), medium (at least two-thirds of the median), and low.

number of vocational disruptions experienced by members of the household (had to start working from home, school or university closed, had to stay home to care for children, had pay or work hours cut, or was laid off). In addition to affecting respondents' availability to protest, this variable is likely to also capture unrelated grievances that may spur people to action. These controls are included in all regressions, except for *work outside home* (which was not asked in the summer 2022 retrospective wave) and *disruptions* (which was not asked in either retrospective wave).

One potential confounder is the availability of nearby protests, which are likely to be more common in population centers. To address this concern, we control for population density (*pop density*) at the ZIP Code level and *residence type* (urban, suburban or rural) at the county level.[40] We also include the *Black pop share* variable described in Section 3.4.4, as protests may be more likely to occur in places with more Black residents. Since protests may also be more likely to occur in wealthier (or poorer) locales, we control for the ZIP Code's *median household income* and *median home value*. Further, it is plausible that there is an ideological slant to the protests' locations, and thus, we include Hillary Clinton's 2016 vote share as well as the combined vote share of the third-party candidates. Finally, to account for any other unobserved sources of regional variation, particularly due to statewide policies, we employed *state* fixed effects.[41] When combining data from multiple waves, we included wave fixed effects as well. Standard errors are clustered at the state level unless noted.

All controls discussed so far are based on data that were either collected before the protests (vote share, census information) or were unlikely to change as a result (e.g., education, income). In our robustness checks in the Online Appendix, we include a second set of controls that bear a greater risk of endogeneity. This set includes *covid*, an indicator of whether anyone in the household had contracted COVID-19 at any point during the pandemic. We asked respondents to report their ideology, ranging from extremely liberal to extremely conservative, on a 7-point scale. However, because ideology is highly correlated with party and because some Black respondents use the "conservative" and "liberal" labels differently (Jefferson 2020), we converted it to a 4-point *ideological extremity* scale ranging from moderate (0) to

---

[40] Based on the National Center for Health Statistics' 2013 Urban-Rural Classification Scheme for counties. Urban corresponds to "large central metro" counties, rural includes "micropolitan" and "noncore" counties, and suburban includes all levels in between. See www.cdc.gov/nchs/data_access/urban_rural.htm.

[41] We chose this strategy because county-level fixed effects drop too many observations, while controlling for the actual locations of protests raises endogeneity concerns.

extremely liberal or conservative (3). Though we think it unlikely that many respondents caught COVID-19 from the protests or became more ideologically extreme due to them, we exclude these variables from the main results to guard against reverse causality.

A common challenge to studying the effects of cross-group friendship is that the number of friendships an individual has with members of a particular out-group likely correlates with their feelings about that group in general. For instance, if non-Black individuals who hold positive attitudes toward Black people are more likely to protest (and also happen to know more Black people), this could generate a spurious correlation between cross-cleavage ties and protest turnout. That is, a correlation between cross-cleavage ties and protests emerges, but it stems from affect toward Black individuals. To address this possibility, we employ a "feeling thermometer" in which respondents rate their feelings toward various racial groups on a scale ranging from cold/unfavorable (0) to warm/favorable (100). We center these variables and divide them by two standard deviations to make them more easily comparable to our binary outcomes (Gelman 2008). We call these *Black favorability, White favorability, Asian favorability,* and *Hispanic favorability.* We do not include these variables in our standard set of controls due to concerns that protesters change their favorability ratings (particularly toward Black people) as a result of attending a protest. However, we draw on them for robustness checks in Section 6, where it is noted, as well as in the Online Appendix.

Analyses were performed with R 4.1.1 statistical computing software. All regressions use ordinary least squares. Topline estimates and crosstabs use survey weights unless reporting the raw number of respondents in a given category.

4 Tie Strength and Mobilization Mechanisms

In this section, we explore Hypothesis 1: tie strength affects how people motivate one another to protest. First, we test whether strong ties to BLM supporters are associated with personal recruitment (i.e., explicitly asking someone you know to protest). Second, we test whether strong ties are necessary for appeals via exposure to social media posts.

4.1 Personal Recruitment

Our most compelling evidence that recruitment relies primarily on strong ties comes from asking protesters who were motivated by a conversation what their relationship was with the other person. When asked about their motivations for protesting, 31 percent of protesters checked the *conversation* option: "someone

Protesters recruited and accompanied by others

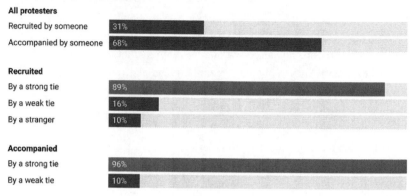

Categories sum to more than 100 percent since the respondents may have been recruited or accompanied by multiple people.

All protesters

Recruited by someone — 31%

Accompanied by someone — 68%

Recruited

By a strong tie — 89%

By a weak tie — 16%

By a stranger — 10%

Accompanied

By a strong tie — 96%

By a weak tie — 10%

Figure 3 Frequency of each level of tie strength between protesters and the people who recruited or accompanied them to protests. Estimates are weighted to census benchmarks

encouraged me, personally, to attend in a message or conversation" (see Figure 3). Of these, 89 percent reported a strong tie with their recruiter(s). Weak ties, in contrast, were involved only 16 percent of the time, and strangers only 10 percent. Strong ties were a mixture of alters in the same household (51 percent) and other households (69 percent).

We also see the role of strong ties when we examine who, if anyone, accompanied the respondent to the protest. Although both individuals could have arrived at their decision to protest independently and then decided to go together, it seems likely that most companions influence one another's decisions. Overall, 68 percent of protesters were accompanied by at least one companion; of these, 96 percent had a strong tie among their companions, while 10 percent had a weak tie. This association is not merely the result of households attending together: 54 percent of those who attended with a strong tie had a companion from their household, while 60 percent had a companion from outside their household. This finding affirms that personal recruitment depends heavily on strong ties.

We see additional evidence for the association between strong ties and recruitment when we examine which protesters became personal recruiters themselves. Overall, 66 percent of protesters reported encouraging someone else to attend. Of these, 86 percent say they were at least partially successful: 69 percent gave an unqualified "yes," while 17 percent said "some" of those they recruited turned out. Although our questionnaire did not drill down on the exact relationship between the respondent and their recruit(s), we can use data from elsewhere in the survey to examine whether protesters with a larger network of strong ties were more likely to recruit others. To do so, we turn to *support tie average*, the number of alters each respondent said they could turn to for assistance (averaged across four types of social support). Those with a *support tie average* in the 20th percentile or below had a 48 percent chance of successfully recruiting someone, while those in the 80th percentile or above had a 64 percent chance. When we regress *recruitment success* on *support tie average* with controls, we find that increasing *support tie average* by 1 tie corresponds to a 1.2 percentage-point increase in the probability of *recruitment success*. This association is substantively modest but statistically significant ($p < 0.001$). Full results can be found in Online Appendix Table A1.

It is worth noting that the number of protesters who claim to have successfully recruited someone else is more than double those who say they were motivated to protest through a conversation. This seeming inconsistency may reflect that many protesters were recruited by multiple alters. Alternatively, recruiters may have overestimated how important their influence was in convincing an alter to show up, or their friends may have downplayed or forgotten some of these conversations. Likewise, roughly twice as many respondents who attended with a *companion* say that someone recruited them through a *conversation*. However, in many cases, the respondent may have recruited the companion rather than the other way around.

Our last piece of evidence comes from the strong non-household ties battery in the June 2020 survey wave. Recall from Section 3.4.2 that respondents could list up to three people outside their household with whom they were closest. Most protesters (56 percent) reported that at least one such alter attended a protest, compared to 6.6 percent of non-protesters. Put another way, if a respondent protested, then, on average, one of their three closest non-household alters was also a protester (mean = 0.97). Thus, protest participation is highly clustered in the social network.

While this clustering is consistent with our hypothesis of direct recruitment among strong ties, we must also account for two other potential mechanisms. First, the strong association between respondents and their alters protesting could be due to homophily. For instance, people with similar political views are more likely to become friends, and a pair of friends could even have met at a prior protest. Alternatively, the association could be due to joint exposure. For instance, they may both find out about a protest from a mutual friend or, if they are neighbors, hear about the same event in their neighborhood.

To distinguish recruitment from homophily and joint exposure, we can examine the frequency of communication. Consider a protester with two friends, one of whom they spoke to every day the week of the protest and the other whom they had not spoken to in a month. If both friends are equally likely to protest, then communication would be irrelevant; their protesting probably arises from joint exposure or mutual interest. However, if the friend they spoke to the week of the protest has a greater probability of protesting, then it seems likely that communication (and hence recruitment) played a role. To make sure that our communication variable is not simply capturing respondents sharing similar interests (and hence, homophily), we control for *habitual communication* (i.e., communication before the pandemic) to isolate the effects of *recent communication*. We account for joint exposure by controlling for whether the alter is a neighbor, coworker, or classmate. In case the frequency of *recent communication* is a proxy for the strength of the relationship (among the three closest alters), we control for the order in which the alters were listed. Finally, we control for whether the alter had COVID-19 as well as our standard respondent-level control variables.

Consistent with our hypothesis, respondents are more likely to protest if an alter also protested, *but only if they communicated recently*. As shown in Online Appendix Table A2, the direct effect of *alter protest* is not statistically significant (and is slightly negative), meaning that the alter's decision to protest and the respondent's decision to protest are unrelated if the two have not communicated in the past week. However, when we look at the interaction between *alter protest* and *recent communication*, we find effects that are positive and significant. Weekly communication with a strong non-household tie protester is associated with an 11 percentage-point increase in the likelihood of protest, while daily communication is associated with a 17 percentage-point increase. Incidentally, *habitual communication* with a protester on a weekly or greater basis is also associated with the respondent protesting, as is having a strong-tie coworker or neighbor attend a protest.

Figure 4 shows the predicted probabilities for each level of *recent communication* with *habitual communication* set to "weekly." On the left side, we see that if the alter did *not* protest, it makes no difference how often they and the respondent communicated. Thus, protesting is not merely a function of being more social. If the alter did protest, however, more frequent communication is associated with an increase in the chances of the respondent protesting from less than 20 percent to nearly 40 percent. Though we do not know what the respondent and their alter talked about, the association between protesting and *recent communication* with a strong-tie protester suggests that at least some of these conversations may have motivated

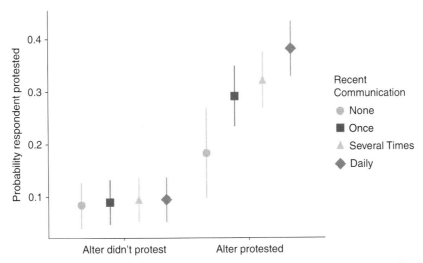

Figure 4 Predicted probability that respondent protested based on protest behavior of their three strongest non-household ties (alters), and frequency with which respondent and alter communicated in the past week. Points represent coefficient estimates from a linear regression with demographic controls (see Online Appendix Table A2). Bars represent 95 percent confidence intervals with standard errors clustered on the respondent

protest turnout.[42] While we cannot make causal claims based on these analyses, the data are consistent with Hypothesis 1 that personal recruitment takes place primarily through strong ties.

4.2 Exposure to Norms, Behavior, and Nonpersonal Appeals

If protest turnout were merely a matter of personal recruitment, we would conclude that strong ties carry the day and that a person's acquaintances are unlikely to have much impact on their odds of protesting. However, personal recruitment was not the means by which most protesters became involved. Only 31 percent of protesters listed *conversation* as a motivation, whereas 51 percent cited *social media*.

We first investigate whether, contrary to our hypothesis, a larger network of strong ties is associated with citing posts on *social media* as a motivation to protest. Beginning with social support ties, we find no statistically significant effect of the *support ties average* on *social media* (see Online Appendix Table A3).

---

[42] The relationship between strong non-household ties and protest motivations is more complex. In a regression predicting which protesters were motivated by *conversation*, the *recent communication × alter protested* interaction term is positive but nonsignificant. It is positive and significant, however, when the outcome's motivations were *conscience* or *faith*.

Moving on to strong non-household ties, we similarly find no association between *alter protest* and respondents citing *social media* as a motivation. Finally, when we interact all the alter traits with *alter protest*, we find that *recent communication* × *alter protest* has no effect (see Online Appendix Table A4). Thus, we find no connection between strong ties and being mobilized through social media. This coheres with Hypothesis 1, concerning ties and social media.

One of the difficulties in measuring the strength of ties associated with social media exposure is that respondents are unlikely to remember where or from whom they learned a given piece of information. Change in perceived norms is even more difficult to pin down since it is likely to come from multiple sources and to develop gradually through repeated exposure. Nevertheless, while users may be poor at estimating how much time they use on a given app (Verbeij et al. 2022), they should be able to recall whether they use a given app *at all*. This allows us to draw inferences about the types of ties involved in the exposure mechanism. As described in Section 3.4.5, we divide these platforms into those in which strong ties are most likely (*messaging platforms*), those likely to be dominated by weak and very weak ties (*following platforms*), and those in between (*friending platforms*).

Figure 5 shows the relationship between using each social media platform and the probability of attending a BLM protest after controlling for demographics (see Online Appendix Table A5). *Messaging* platforms have no association with protest. Facebook, the sole *friending* platform, has a negative association. All else being equal, Facebook users are about half a percentage point less likely to protest ($p < 0.1$). Most *following* platforms, on the other hand, are positively associated with protest.[43] Thus, except for YouTube, platforms with a greater proportion of weak ties tend to be the ones positively associated with protest. Within the set of respondents who protested, weak tie platforms are associated with the *social media* motivation (see Online Appendix Table A6). There are limitations to this approach – we do not know, for instance, whether exposure through these sites is coming from close friends, acquaintances, or strangers – but on the whole, these results suggest that the exposure mechanism operates primarily through weak ties. And, more clearly, strong ties are not the key as posited by Hypothesis 1 (i.e., mobilization via social media exposure does not depend on strong ties).

We further observe notable differences among weak-tie social media. For instance, TikTok use is especially likely to be associated with protesting, even

---

[43] Apps such as Twitter and Instagram may also have somewhat higher rates of Democrats and Black Americans compared to the general population (see www.pewresearch.org/internet/fact-sheet/social-media/?menuItem=2fc5fff9-9899–4317-b786-9e0b60934bcf and www.pewresearch.org/internet/2019/04/24/sizing-up-twitter-users/).

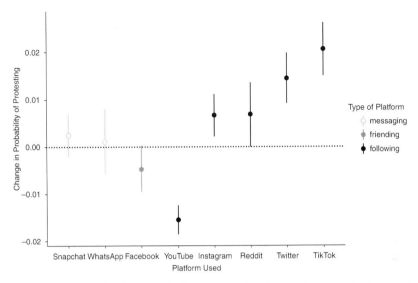

Figure 5 Association between being a user of each social media platform and the probability of attending a BLM protest. Points represent coefficient estimates for each platform based on linear regression with demographic controls (see Online Appendix Table A5). Bars represent 95 percent confidence intervals

compared to other *following* platforms (and after controlling for respondent age and other demographics). This is consistent with contemporaneous reporting on the use of the platform by BLM protesters (Janfaza 2020). Previous research has suggested that Musical.ly (a prior iteration of TikTok) was an important site for political expression in 2016 despite its small user base at the time (Literat and Kligler-Vilenchik 2019). Scholars examining the link between participation in demonstrations and social media use across national contexts report that using TikTok is associated with considerably higher odds of protesting, controlling for demographics and political leanings (Boulianne and Lee 2022). Similar to our results, they find the same was not true of YouTube, even though it is another weak-tie, video-based platform. Boulianne and Lee (2022) hypothesize that TikTok users are especially predisposed toward alternative forms of polit-ical participation and using the platform for collective action.

4.3 Implications

While causal mechanisms are notoriously difficult to establish (especially as protesters themselves may not be fully aware of the motivations behind their actions), our findings are consistent with a scenario where a combination of weak and strong ties operating through different mechanisms came together to produce collective action. Over a quarter (27 percent) of protesters in our data reported they were motivated to attend a BLM event through personal recruitment in a conversation with a strong tie. Having close ties to other protesters with whom one had communicated frequently and recently was also a notable predictor of joining the movement.

Conversely, over half of all protesters cited seeing posts from people they knew on social media as a motivation to attend. Higher use of social media apps that facilitate weaker ties (*following platforms*) was also associated with protesting, while higher use of apps associated with (comparatively) strong ties (*messaging platforms*) was not.

These patterns align with past research suggesting that different types of social contacts have different roles to play during mobilization for collective action. Walgrave and Ketelaars (2019), for instance, find that strong and weak ties were relevant at different stages of the process. The companions with whom protesters showed up to an event tended to be strong ties, whereas the contacts to provide information about the event's existence were often weak. Similarly, in our data, the overwhelming majority of those who attended protests *with* others had at least one strong tie accompanying them. In contrast, information acquisition and persuasion could happen through exposure to public social media posts (ostensibly dominated by weak ties) rather than through strong-tie one-on-one recruitment.[44]

What do these findings about tie strength imply for social movements going forward? The unusualness of the pandemic cannot be overstated: we simply cannot know if social media ties would have mattered as much in a hypothetical world in which COVID-19 did not exist. That said, this is certainly not the first protest where social media played an important role, and we have a particularly comprehensive view of the role that social networks and social media interplayed to mobilize circa 2020. Our results suggest that, over time, we may be witnessing a global shift in recruiting patterns as digital platforms offer exposure to larger numbers of weaker-tie social contacts.

5 Movement Insiders and Outsiders

The massive size of the BLM protests meant that, by definition, they included many protesters who had not participated in BLM previously. The 2020 BLM

---

[44] Compared to Walgrave and Ketelaars' (2019) study fielded during demonstrations in eight countries from 2009 to 2014, we see the BLM protests relied somewhat less on personal invitations from strong ties (27 percent vs. 43 percent–48 percent). Part of the reason may be shifting social media usage away from Facebook and toward *following* platforms among younger people, who are more likely than older people to protest.

protests drew what we call "outsiders" – people who had never participated in any protest for any cause before. Understanding how and why these outsiders came to protest is vital to isolating how such large movements emerge. We have argued that mobilization works very differently for outsiders and "insiders" (those who have protested against racism or police violence in the past) due to the networks in which they are embedded. Specifically, we predicted variation in the mobilizer, mechanism, social embeddedness, and affective driver.[45]

5.1 Mobilizer Characteristics and Mechanisms

We predicted in Hypothesis 2 that insiders would be mobilized by other insiders, and outsiders would be relatively less so. We test this with a question that asked protesters to describe who had the biggest influence on their decision to attend, a role we refer to as a *mobilizer*. Unlike the recruiter question, this item was shown to all protesters regardless of whether they cited *conversation* as a motivation. While some mobilizers may have explicitly *recruited* respondents, others may have *inspired* them to do so – for instance, by sharing stories about a time when they were victimized or posting a photo of themselves at a protest. In Figure 6, we compare how insiders and outsiders responded to six questions about the identity of their mobilizer.

As seen in Figure 6, insiders are more likely to say their mobilizer was a self-identified activist or prior protester. Our regression results confirm these associations (see Online Appendix Table B1). All else being equal, insiders were 16 percentage points more likely to be mobilized by an activist and 18 percentage points more likely to be mobilized by a prior protester.[46] Both findings are statistically significant at $p < 0.001$. Furthermore, the fact that outsiders were mobilized relatively less by insiders suggests that if someone did indeed mobilize them, it was more likely to be an outsider (although we cannot definitively conclude that).

In Section 2, we predicted that social media exposure would be a more common mobilization mechanism for insiders. For those who already believe

---

[45] Throughout this section, we use the main dataset collected between June and November 2020. However, since the insider/outsider question asked if the respondent had attended a protest prior to the past month, it is possible that some respondents surveyed later in the year said yes in reference to BLM protests they had attended in June. Therefore, in the appendix, we run two robustness checks. First, we limit the data to the June 2020 wave, which ended about a month after the murder of George Floyd. Second, we examine data from the December retrospective wave, which asked about protests attended "before this year." Since respondents would probably be less likely to remember who mobilized them five months later, we limited this question to people who recalled someone personally recruiting them. The results mostly agree in direction, though some are no longer statistically significant, which we suspect is due to the smaller sample.

[46] We did not ask whether this person was a prior *BLM* protester/activist, but given the circumstances, it seems safe to assume that most of them were.

Mobilizer characteristics for movement insiders and outsiders

Percentage of movement insiders (black) and outsiders (gray) who report specific mobilizer/mobilization characteristics.

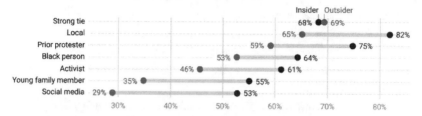

Figure 6 Attributes of the mobilizer who had the biggest impact on the respondent's decision to protest. All insider-outsider differences are significant at the $p < 0.001$ level except for *strong tie* (not significant). Estimates are weighted to census benchmarks

in the cause and have experience attending protests, a brief exposure should be sufficient to prompt the social utility that pushes insiders (e.g., seeing that friends are attending). Alternatively, they may already want to attend and simply need to know where and when protests are happening. Our predictions are borne out in Figure 6. As predicted, insiders were far more likely to say that their mobilizer had influenced them through *social media*. In the regression model, the difference is smaller – 15 percentage points – but still significant at $p < 0.05$ after controlling for other factors (see Online Appendix Table B1).

While not directly relevant to our hypotheses, Figure 6 also shows that outsiders were less likely to say their mobilizer was *local* (within an hour's drive) or a *young family member* (under age thirty). These findings may speak to our household prediction (that outsiders are recruited more by those outside their household), but we will test that more directly in the next section.[47] We also find that insiders were slightly more likely to be influenced by someone who was Black. This may also reflect that other insiders for this movement are relatively likely to be Black.

Overall, the data offer strong confirmation of our expectations regarding the key type of mobilizer and the key mechanism. Insiders are more likely to act because of other insiders who urge them on via social media.

5.2 Social Embeddedness

Part of the reason for the different patterns of mobilization we observe is that insiders and outsiders are embedded in different social contexts. Consider a respondent's three closest non-household alters, whom we asked questions

---

[47] Those in the household are by definition local and more likely to be relatives that are young.

Ties between protesters and their recruiters

Percentage of movement insiders (black) and outsiders (gray) who report having a certain type of tie with their protest recruiter.

	Insider	Outsider
Strong tie (Household)	61%	30%
Strong tie (Non-household)	53%	71%
Weak tie	15%	16%
Stranger	11%	8%

Figure 7 Strength and type of ties between protesters and their recruiters, if any. Estimates are weighted to census benchmarks

about in the June 2020 wave. Most insiders (63 percent) reported that at least one of these people had been to a protest. Moreover, 38 percent of insiders said that at least two of these alters had protested, and 22 percent reported that all three had. While we do not know whether all three alters knew each other, it seems likely that many, perhaps most, of these respondents were embedded in social circles where protest was commonplace. Among outsiders, in contrast, less than half (46 percent) said that any of their three closest non-household alters had protested, 17 percent said that at least two had, and only 9 percent said all three had. Among non-protesters, nearly all of whom were outsiders,[48] only 7 percent said one of their alters protested, 2 percent said at least two had, and less than 1 percent said all three did. These differences are statistically significant ($p < 0.01$) and remain so when controlling for demographics (see Online Appendix Table B4). Thus, outsiders, in addition to never before having attended a BLM protest, are less likely to be surrounded by a circle of protest-inclined family and friends.

Insiders are not merely more likely to socialize with groups of protesters; they are also more likely to live with them. We test this with a survey item that asked those who were recruited via conversations to describe their *recruiter*. The results in Figure 7 show, as expected, that insiders were far more likely to be recruited by someone within their household (intra-household), while outsiders were more likely to be recruited through a strong non-household tie (inter-household). These results are confirmed in our regression analyses (Online Appendix Table B3), where we find that insiders are 14 percentage points more likely than outsiders to report being recruited by a strong household tie ($p < 0.01$). Conversely, outsiders are 7 percentage points more likely to have

---

[48] Given that most Americans were not previously involved in BLM, we can conclude that relatively few non-protesters were insiders. Some insiders may have missed out because of illness or work, but given that we were asking about protests over an entire month, it seems unlikely that this category was very large. Of course, some fraction may have also become disillusioned or lost interest.

been recruited by a strong non-household tie ($p < 0.01$). Thus, the difference between insiders' and outsiders' mobilization is not so much a matter of tie strength but rather a matter of tie embeddedness, "within" versus "between" households. In sum, insiders are more likely than outsiders to be motivated by people *within* their household. This likely reflects both social influence and shared values among those who live and/or spend much time together.

Together, these results show that outsiders are less embedded in a close-knit network of protesters and protest recruiters than insiders are. Moreover, as discussed in Section 5.1, when somebody does mobilize them, this person is less likely to live nearby. All of this suggests that, when recruited by a personal conversation, outsiders are more likely to be mobilized through a "bridge" to a particular mobilizer with whom they do not share a lot of mutual alters, while insiders are more likely to be mobilized through the interconnected milieu of friends and family they live among and regularly see.[49]

Every survey respondent who said they attended a protest was asked to report their motivation for doing so (see Section 3.2 for question wording). The percentages of insiders and outsiders citing each motivation are presented in Figure 8. Most of these results affirm our hypothesis that insiders and outsiders are motivated through different channels as a result of the networks in which they are already embedded. For instance, insiders were far more likely than outsiders to cite *organizational motivations*. Specifically, insiders were about twice as likely to cite *membership* in an organization (17 percent vs. 9 percent), as befits their insider status. They were also twice as likely to cite being contacted by an organizer (15 percent vs. 7 percent), an unambiguous "insider tie." Overall, over a quarter (27 percent) of insiders cited one of these two organizational motivations, compared to only 14 percent of outsiders. These results also hold up when controlling for other factors in a regression (see Online Appendix Tables B5–7). Thus, according to protesters' recollections, movement insiders appear to have played a larger role in mobilizing their fellow insiders than in mobilizing first-time protesters from the outside. This is further confirmation for our hypothesized insider mobilizers (i.e., other insiders).

Further, consistent with our theory about mechanisms and evidence presented earlier in Section 5.1, insiders were far more likely than outsiders to

---

[49] We also find in a regression that insiders are 9 percentage points more likely ($p < 0.01$) to say the person who recruited them in a message or conversation was a stranger (see Online Appendix Table B3). Although we cannot be sure, we suspect this finding is evidence of outreach from organizations, yet another form of insiders' connections to other insiders. Moreover, it makes sense that insiders are more likely than outsiders to be persuaded by an appeal from a complete stranger to attend a protest. Most insiders do not need to be convinced of the importance of the cause or the efficacy of protest; a small nudge from the organizers, along with the details of the event, may suffice.

Motivations reported by movement insiders and outsiders

Percentage of movement insiders (black) and outsiders (gray) who report
specific motivations for attending a BLM protest.

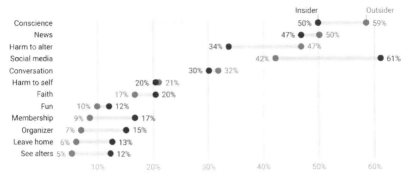

Figure 8 Motivations for attending a protest in movement insiders versus
outsiders. Insider-outsider differences are significant at the *p* < 0.001 level
except for *faith* (*p* < 0.01), *news* and *fun* (*p* < 0.1), and *harm to self* and
conversation (not significant). Estimates are weighted to census benchmarks

cite *social media* as a motivation (61 percent versus 42 percent). When controlling
for other variables, the gap between them is smaller (12 percentage points) but still
significant (*p* < 0.001). Even though they may be less influential than interpersonal
communication, social media posts still offer enough of an incentive to prompt
insiders. This pattern again suggests that insiders may not need detailed persuasive
appeals, but rather just coordinating information and signals from social contacts
of the potential benefits of protesting.

5.3 Affective Drivers

Figure 8 allows us to explore our prediction that insiders – embedded in a social
network full of protest-goers – would be drawn to protest by opportunities to
socialize. This is perhaps an ironic expectation given one may expect a priori
that insiders are more devoted to the cause than outsiders and, thus, less likely to
protest for self-serving social reasons. Yet, the reality is that social movements
also play a crucial community-building role with members wanting to maintain
connections to one another.

We find strong support for our hypothesis that the affective driver for insiders
involves social utility; they were more likely to cite *see alters* ("Wanted to see
people I know in person") than were outsiders (12 percent versus 5 percent).
Relatedly, it seems likely that the *leave home* motivation ("Wanted a reason to
leave the house"), which is substantially greater for insiders (13 percent versus 6
percent), was driven in large part by a desire to socialize with non-household

alters. Indeed, in most jurisdictions, prior COVID-19 lockdowns had prevented people from gathering but not from leaving their homes altogether. Regression results show smaller gaps: – 4 and 3 percentage points, respectively ($p < 0.001$). These gaps are still substantial, however, given how few respondents cited these motivations.[50] In sum, insiders seemed more likely to report social reasons (i.e., wanting to connect with other people). Even if these alters did not explicitly recruit them, their expected presence at the protest(s) was itself mobilizing.

Outsiders may have fewer opportunities to see friends at a protest, but they are more susceptible to another form of mobilization: moral shocks. Because they are new to the cause, we predicted that outsiders are more likely to be stirred to action by watching the news, hearing stories of racism from alters, or appeals to their consciences. Insiders may find such appeals moving as well, but they are less novel. Is such novelty important? The results are mixed. In Figure 8, we see that outsiders are more likely than insiders to say they were motivated by *conscience* (59 percent versus 50 percent) or *harm to alter* (47 percent versus 34 percent). The difference in *news* (50 percent versus 47 percent) is in the expected direction but is not statistically significant.[51]

Thanks to the networks they are embedded in, insiders are more likely to be mobilized by the promise of the experience, while outsiders need to be swayed by the tenor of the movement itself. Of course, successful movements might convert outsiders to insiders, enabling future collective actions. It is thus important to stimulate actions via social pressure and utility in addition to regularly appealing to substantive motives when the shock eventually wears off.

We thus have evidence for our affective driver predictions. Earlier in the section, we offered data in support of our mechanism prediction for insiders: social media exposure was key. Here, we test the outsider mobilization mechanism, and this is one prediction where the evidence is lacking. In contrast to our expectation that outsiders are more likely to be mobilized via conversations/ personal recruitment, Figure 8 shows no significant difference between insiders and outsiders when it comes to conversations. This may reflect a tension in our hypothesis insofar as we expect and find intra-household mobilization to occur more for insiders than outsiders. Such intra-household mobilization might involve longer conversations simply because the individuals know one another well, meaning we find conversations/personal recruitment present in the data for

---

[50] While some respondents may have been ashamed to report self-serving motivations, we do not have reason to think that this social desirability bias should have been substantially weaker among insiders.

[51] These gaps disappear and even reverse when controlling for other variables (see Online Appendix Tables B5–7). Nevertheless, we can say that while being an outsider does not make one more likely to name a moral-shock-related motivation, these motivations seem to have spurred more outsiders overall.

both insiders and outsiders. Unfortunately, we do not have the data to differentiate the mechanism of recruitment holding the mobilizer and social setting constant.

5.4 Leaderless Movements and Last-Mile Mobilization

Our data confirm our hypotheses: insiders and outsiders were mobilized through distinct channels, and it is thus crucial to understand those varying routes to collective action. Insiders were more likely to be mobilized by other insiders, through social media ties, and motivated by the social utility of protesting. This motivation also included the utility of sharing the experience with members of their households or their three closest non-household ties; this is similar to what motivates many soldiers in war – that is, they partially fight for one another (Wong 2003). To be clear, we do not mean to minimize the role that values and the pursuit of justice play among insiders; it remains one of the most important motivations they cite, much more so than social drivers. Rather, we suggest that moral drivers had become ingrained, and thus turning out for another protest also depended on the appeal of spending time with friends who shared these values.

Even so, the summer 2020 protests could only have occurred at such a massive scale by also bringing in outsiders. Many of these outsiders came out because they were mobilized via ties outside of their households. Outsiders were also more likely than insiders to protest due to moral shock, such as harm to someone they knew. The bottom line is that outsiders showed up for reasons that did not, on the surface, link as strongly back to movement organizations. Yet, in a larger sense, organizations still played a crucial role, having worked for years to set the stage for outsiders to recognize their moral obligations and ties to victims as reasons to act. The murder of George Floyd did not occur in a vacuum but was yet another brutal killing of a Black person, and vigorous advocacy for these victims surely was crucial to stimulating outsiders. Put another way, this moral shock was not a singular event but the culmination of recurring injustices to which organizations and insiders brought attention.

We emphasize this point to make clear that, despite our focus on social networks and social media, we do not mean to diminish the role of civic organizations and organizing. Our work points to important distinctions between the practices of mobilizing (i.e., providing people with the impetus to gather and complete tasks) and organizing (the cyclical process through which constituencies learn to be self-governing). Organizers help people make strategic choices about how best to channel their voices through collective action. And while organizing can lead to mobilization, it is a distinct concept.

Moreover, the work of Michener, Han, Small, and others rightly notes that the discursive frameworks used to mobilize people on social media are often designed – and even gatekept – by grassroots organizations, and BLM is no exception (Han, McKenna, and Oyakawa 2021; Michener 2020; Small 2009). This point about organizations playing important roles is one to which we are sensitive (see Tufekci 2017); there are certainly other approaches to mobilization where more organizational structure is essential. That said, it is clear to us that the racial reckonings of 2020 are a case study about how mobilization *can* now occur without a heavy reliance on organizing under some conditions. This is a social movement dynamic that would not have been possible in prior decades.

6 Beyond the Contact Hypothesis: Mobilizing Allies

Our survey, as well as others, finds that a majority of protesters were White (e.g., Barroso and Minkin 2020; Fisher 2020). Specifically, we estimate that 52 percent of protesters were White, 22 percent were Black, 17 percent were Hispanic, and 6 percent were Asian, with the rest identifying with other races or opting not to identify with just one race. Although non-Black adults protested at about half the rate of Black adults (4 percent versus 8 percent), this turnout is nonetheless remarkable given that the protest was largely on behalf of Black people. What role did Black adults play in mobilizing millions of non-Black protesters?

6.1 Racial Homophily

We begin with some descriptive data to lay out the context for cross-cleavage (Black/non-Black) mobilization. One of the more consistent findings in social networks research is that Americans tend to form ties with same-race alters, a phenomenon known as racial homophily (Marsden 1988; Smith, McPherson, and Smith-Lovin 2014). This tendency is particularly pronounced for strong ties (McPherson, Smith-Lovin, and Cook 2001). Our data support this finding. In the summer 2022 retrospective wave, we reintroduced the strong non-household ties battery, this time asking each respondent about the racial identity of each alter. The results are displayed in Table 4, showing the percentage of respondents who listed at least one member of a given race among their alters. In the first row, for instance, we see that 75 percent of Asian respondents listed at least one Asian alter, 15 percent listed a Black alter, and so forth.[52]

Looking along the diagonal, we can see the rate of racial homophily by group among the closest three non-household ties: 75 percent of Asian respondents named an Asian alter, 88 percent of Black respondents named a Black alter,

---

[52] In this wave, respondents could list multiple races. A respondent who identifies as both Black and Hispanic, for instance, would be included in both the second and third rows.

Table 4 Percentage of respondents with an alter of each race among their three
strongest non-household ties

Respondent Race	Asian Alter	Black Alter	Hispanic Alter	White Alter	Other Alter	No Alters
Asian	75%	16%	13%	48%	10%	4%
Black	7%	88%	14%	22%	8%	4%
Hispanic	9%	17%	77%	54%	5%	3%
White	5%	10%	12%	92%	5%	5%
Other	12%	22%	18%	63%	47%	8%
Average respondent	10%	22%	21%	72%	7%	4%
Expected percentage if ties were random	18%	33%	41%	91%	18%	4%

77 percent of Hispanic respondents named a Hispanic alter, and 92 percent of
White respondents named a White alter. Asian, Black, and Hispanic respondents
named a White alter more than any other group besides their own. The trend is
likely a result of the fact that there are more White people in the population with
whom to make connections.[53] Conversely, residential segregation is partly respon-
sible for Black and White people having such high levels of homophily. Low rates
of intermarriage between Black and White people (Fryer 2007) and social norms
against identifying as both races likely also contribute to the low rates of Black
people and White people citing one another as alters.

The final row of the table shows what proportion of Americans would have
a tie to someone of each respective race if there was no social segregation or
homophily – that is, if ties were random. Although only 14 percent of the US
population identified as Black on the 2020 census, we should expect 33 percent
of Americans to have a Black strong-non-household alter if ties were random,
since every respondent has three opportunities to name a Black person.[54] Instead,
we find that only 10 percent of White people, 16 percent of Asian people, and
17 percent of Hispanic people have a Black strong-non-household alter. The

---

[53] Members of the "other" race category – which includes large numbers of Native Americans –
name White alters more often than they name alters whose race is "other." This may be because
many of them are living in predominantly White communities or they identify with multiple
races.

[54] See Online Appendix C to know how this statistic was calculated.

average Black person, in turn, has far fewer ties than expected at random to every other group. This lack of cross-cleavage ties could pose a significant barrier to mobilization if the people most affected by the problems BLM seeks to remedy – Black people – have limited connections to the rest of the population.

6.2 The Impact of Strong Cross-Cleavage Ties

These descriptive data mean cross-cleavage ties are relatively scarce. Yet, we predicted in Hypothesis 3 that they would be powerful, with non-Black individuals being more likely to protest due to ties with Black individuals relative to ties with non-Black individuals.[55] In Table 5, we report regressions of *protest* (whether the respondent protested) on *Black strong n-hh ties* (how many of the respondent's strong non-household ties are Black). In addition to the standard demographic control variables, each model controls for the total number of strong non-household ties of any race (*strong n-hh ties*), since not everyone listed three people.[56] Even-numbered models include additional controls as a robustness check: *covid, ideological extremity,* and *favorability* toward each racial/ethnic group (the warmth of respondent's feelings toward that group). We run each model with and without these controls, since, unlike the demographic controls, they are potentially endogenous (e.g., respondents could have caught COVID-19 at a protest or become ideologically more radical as a result of clashes with police).

Models 1–4 show the results for Black respondents. Models 1–2 indicate that Black people with more Black alters among their strong non-household ties are not more likely to protest. However, Models 3–4 show that Black people who have *any* Black alters are more likely to protest than those who have none. A possible interpretation is that Black people who are disconnected from the Black community are less inclined to protest on behalf of it. On the other hand, provided at least one alter is Black, the races of the other alters do not make protest more or less likely.

Models 5–8 show non-Black respondents. In Model 5, we see that for each Black alter named, non-Black respondents are 8 percentage points more likely to protest. This association remains significant in Model 6 when we control for *Black favorability* and other attitudinal factors. This robustness indicates that it really is ties to Black individuals – not merely diffuse exposure to Black people,

---

[55] We acknowledge the potential measurement issue contained within this expectation – given that White people, in particular, may overestimate friendship ties to Black people – while also noting that such patterns comport with a robust literature on "imagined contact effects" (see, e.g., Crisp and Turner 2009; Miles and Crisp 2014).

[56] The first question in this section asked respondents to type in the initials of up to three alters. In total, 91 percent of respondents listed three alters, 2 percent listed two, 3 percent listed one, and 4 percent did not list any. Among the latter, an unknown number may have simply not wished to answer the question.

Table 5 Association between protesting and strong non-household (n-hh) ties. For additional results, see Online Appendix Tables C1–5

Dependent Variable:			protest					
		Black			Non-Black			
Model:	(1)	(2)	(3)	(4)	(5)	(6)	(7)	(8)
Variables								
Black strong n-hh ties	0.01	0.02			0.08***	0.07***		
	(0.03)	(0.03)			(0.02)	(0.02)		
any Black strong n-hh ties			0.17*	0.21**			0.09***	0.09***
			(0.09)	(0.10)			(0.03)	(0.03)
strong n-hh ties	0.01	−0.02	−0.02	−0.05	0.02	0.007	0.02	0.007
	(0.03)	(0.03)	(0.04)	(0.04)	(0.01)	(0.01)	(0.01)	(0.01)
Black favorability		−0.10		−0.12		0.09***		0.09***
		(0.07)		(0.08)		(0.03)		(0.03)
ideological extremity		0.01		0.02		0.07***		0.07***
		(0.03)		(0.03)		(0.007)		(0.007)
covid		0.0001		−0.005		0.06***		0.06***
		(0.06)		(0.06)		(0.01)		(0.01)
Favorability (other races)		Yes		Yes		Yes		Yes
Demographic Controls	Yes	Yes	Yes	Yes	Yes	Yes	Yes	Yes
Fixed-effects								
state	Yes	Yes	Yes	Yes	Yes	Yes	Yes	Yes
Fit statistics								
Observations	362	344	362	344	2,449	2,396	2,449	2,396
Squared Correlation	0.35873	0.37971	0.36719	0.39030	0.28206	0.33227	0.28133	0.33179
Pseudo R²	0.36199	0.38916	0.37281	0.40320	0.28702	0.34809	0.28614	0.34746
BIC	713.57	719.27	708.76	713.35	2,640.2	2,473.7	2,642.7	2,475.5

Clustered (state) standard-errors in parentheses
*Signif. Codes: ***: 0.01, **: 0.05, *: 0.1*

general goodwill, or some other factor – that drives protest. Models 7 and 8 confirm this finding, showing that non-Black people with *any* ties to Black people among their three strongest non-household alters are 9 percentage points more likely to protest than those with none.

In sum, we see that cross-cleavage ties to Black people increase the probability of protest for non-Blacks. Our use of the term "cross-cleavage" rather than "cross-racial" is deliberate. We see no significant effect for the percentage of Hispanic or Asian alters on White respondents, for example (see Online Appendix Tables C4–5). Although there are other racial and ethnic fault lines in American society, the primary cleavage associated with the 2020 racial justice protests was between Black and non-Black people, particularly Black people and White people. Therefore, strong ties that bridge this cleavage are the ones that matter most. Moreover, the direction of the tie matters. If Black protesters with non-Black alters were also more likely to protest, we might conclude that the type of people who form cross-cleavage relationships are more likely to be activists and hence more likely to attend protests. However, as shown in Online Appendix Tables C3–5, there is no significant association between a Black person's decision to protest and the number of White, Asian, or Hispanic alters they have.[57] This non-finding is consistent with our hypothesis that Black people are mobilizing their White alters and not merely that the sorts of Black people and White people who befriend one another are both more inclined to protest in the first place. In short, this is clear evidence for the first part of Hypothesis 3, that non-Black individuals are more likely to protest due to ties with Black individuals.

6.3 Cross-Cleavage Mobilization and Tie Strength

We suggested that cross-cleavage mobilization can occur via strong or weak ties. That said, even though we did not formally predict it, there may be reason to expect mobilization to be more impactful in the presence of strong ties: the emotional attachment that comes with strong ties might lead non-Black individuals to act on behalf of those whom they care about. We can test this with a question from our summer 2022 survey that asked respondents about their non-household ties: we asked non-Black respondents if they had *any* ties to Black people whom they had known for more than three years (i.e., since before the pandemic and the murder of George Floyd). Those who said yes were asked if these Black people were acquaintances, friends, or family (see Section 3.4.4 for exact wording).

---

[57] On the contrary, White respondents with more ingroup ties to other White people are less likely to protest. Curiously, however, Asian and "other race" respondents are significantly *more* likely to protest if they have more ties to White alters ($p<0.05$).

Percentage respondents with cross-cleavage ties by race

Percentage of respondents who reported having at least one cross-cleavage tie of each type since before the COVID-19 pandemic started. Black respondents were asked about ties with non-Black people; all other respondents were asked about ties with Black people.

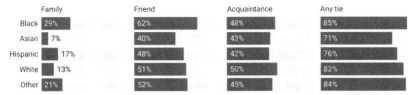

Figure 9 Percentage of respondents with at least one cross-cleavage tie of a given type

As shown in Figure 9, respondents reported few cross-cleavage family ties, but considerably more friendship and acquaintance ties.[58] We assume friends and family connote stronger ties than acquaintances, though they may not always be as strong as the top three non-household ties discussed in Sections 6.1–6.2.

We next look to see the impact of these relationships on protesting, with regressions displayed in Table 6. For Black people (Models 1–2), we see that, as predicted, neither strong nor weak cross-cleavage ties are associated with protesting. For non-Black people (Models 3–4), strong cross-cleavage ties (friends and family) are associated with protest, but weak ties (acquaintances) are not.

6.4 Sharing Stories with Non-Black Friends

Over a third of non-Black protesters (39 percent) cited *harm to alter* ("Someone I knew was a victim of racism and/or police violence") as a motivation for protesting. Those who did were especially likely to say that the person who had the biggest impact on their decision to attend (i.e., their mobilizer) was Black. Table 7 shows that non-Black people (Models 3–4) were 17–19 percentage points more likely to say a Black person had the biggest impact on them if *harm to alter* was among their motivations. For Black respondents (Models 1–2), however, there does not appear to be any relationship. A reasonable interpretation is that when Black people took the initiative to share their stories with non-Black people, it made a major impression on them – so much so that these

---

[58] As discussed, these responses are more likely to be influenced by social desirability bias than the non-household strong ties questions, where respondents were asked to pre-commit to three particular alters by writing down their initials before they knew they would be asked about race. Nevertheless, these percentages do not seem unreasonable. Perhaps what is more striking is that 20 percent of respondents could not recall maintaining any cross-cleavage ties for more than three years.

Table 6 Association between protest and having strong and weak cross-cleavage ties. For additional results, see Online Appendix Table C6

Dependent Variable:	protest			
	Black		Non-Black	
Model:	(1)	(2)	(3)	(4)
Variables				
non-Black weak tie	−0.01	−0.01		
	(0.008)	(0.008)		
Black weak tie			−0.005	−0.01
			(0.01)	(0.01)
non-Black strong tie	0.01	0.01		
	(0.01)	(0.01)		
Black strong tie			0.05**	0.04*
			(0.02)	(0.02)
Black favorability		0.001		0.06***
		(0.01)		(0.01)
ideological extremity		0.005		0.06***
		(0.004)		(0.006)
covid		−0.0005		0.05***
		(0.010)		(0.01)
Demographic Controls	Yes	Yes	Yes	Yes
Favorability (other races)		Yes		Yes
Fixed-effects				
state	Yes	Yes	Yes	Yes
Fit statistics				
Observations	2,253	2,157	3,880	3,783
Squared Correlation	0.07359	0.08042	0.21773	0.26644
Pseudo R^2	−0.23089	−0.24737	0.30975	0.38616
BIC	−339.12	−290.13	2,775.9	2,555.2

Clustered (state) standard-errors in parentheses
Signif. Codes: ***: 0.01, **: 0.05, *: 0.1

respondents cited the story sharer as their top mobilizer. Within the Black community, however, stories of victimization were just one of many tools used to mobilize one another, and they were no more effective than other tools like peer pressure or providing logistical details. For non-Black respondents, especially those less familiar with prejudice firsthand, hearing a story of victimization was more likely to be novel and provide a moral shock.

We have evidence that the ties connecting Black story-sharers to non-Black protesters are likely to be strong. Returning to our social support ties (as described in Section 3.4.3, the number people on whom one can rely for social support), in Table 8 we regress *harm to alter* on *support ties average*. The association is positive and significant ($p < 0.01$), showing that strong ties are correlated with this form of mobilization. Each additional support alter increases the probability of citing this motivation by 1 percentage point. Granted, our ability to perform inference with this variable is limited because higher numbers of strong ties may also be correlated with higher numbers of

Table 7 *Black mobilizer* regressed on *harm to alter* and other motivations. For additional results, see Online Appendix Table C7

Dependent Variable: respondent race	Black		non-Black	
Model:	(1)	(2)	(3)	(4)
Variables				
harm to alter	0.006	−0.01	0.17***	0.15***
	(0.03)	(0.03)	(0.02)	(0.02)
Black favorability		0.13***		0.10***
		(0.04)		(0.03)
ideological extremity		−0.010		−0.008
		(0.009)		(0.009)
covid		−0.003		0.06**
		(0.04)		(0.02)
Demographic Controls	Yes	Yes	Yes	Yes
Favorability (other races)		Yes		Yes
Fixed-effects				
state	Yes	Yes	Yes	Yes
wave	Yes	Yes	Yes	Yes
Fit statistics				
Observations	918	882	3,584	3,492
Squared Correlation	0.15696	0.18803	0.10949	0.12338
Pseudo R^2	0.17426	0.21460	0.07986	0.09069
BIC	1,397.7	1,364.1	5,623.1	5,491.4

Clustered (state) standard-errors in parentheses
Signif. Codes: ***: 0.01, **: 0.05, *: 0.1

weak ones. The overall picture is that moral shock stimulated non-Black protesters and that motivation was possibly facilitated by having strong support networks.

How common was story-sharing, and by what medium were these stories of victimization shared? Our summer 2022 survey wave allowed for some tentative answers. Respondents in the cross-cleavage ties battery were asked if one of the Black people they knew had encouraged them to protest and if so, whether they had done so in a "personal message or conversation" or "by posting to social media." We then asked if one of them "told you stories about racism they have faced" and presented the same response options. The percentages from protesters and non-protesters are displayed in Figure 10.

Unfortunately, it is difficult to recover what the differences actually were at the time because those who did not follow through and protest are more liable to forget, and social media posts may be less memorable than a conversation. Moreover, stories of racism could have been shared following a protest rather than before. Still, this question is informative to the extent that it gives us a lower bound on how commonplace sharing personal accounts of racism has become. A majority of Black respondents report having shared stories with non-Black

Table 8 The probability of a respondent citing *harm to alter* as a motivation for protesting, regressed on the number of people they can rely on for important forms of social support (*support ties average*). For additional results, see Online Appendix Table C8

Dependent Variable: respondent race Model:	harm to alter			
	Black		non-Black	
	(1)	(2)	(3)	(4)
Variables				
support ties average	0.01**	0.01*	0.01***	0.01***
	(0.007)	(0.007)	(0.004)	(0.004)
Black favorability		0.05		0.11***
		(0.04)		(0.03)
ideological extremity		−0.009		0.004
		(0.02)		(0.008)
covid		−0.07		−0.04**
		(0.05)		(0.02)
Favorability (other races)		Yes		Yes
Demographic Controls	Yes	Yes	Yes	Yes
Fixed-effects				
state	Yes	Yes	Yes	Yes
wave	Yes	Yes	Yes	Yes
Fit statistics				
Observations	878	845	3,409	3,326
Squared Correlation	0.22699	0.23895	0.24563	0.26304
Pseudo R^2	0.17725	0.18793	0.19687	0.21281
BIC	1,632.1	1,617.0	4,660.1	4,541.6

Clustered (state) standard-errors in parentheses
*Signif. Codes: ***: 0.01, **: 0.05, *: 0.1*

alters, regardless of whether they attended a protest themselves (Figure 10, top). Similarly, the vast majority of non-Black protesters – and, remarkably, nearly half (45 percent) of non-Black people who did *not* protest – recall hearing stories of racism from their Black alters. Given that, as shown in Section 6.3, very few non-Black people have a Black strong non-household tie, this high a rate of personal disclosure is impressive. Black people may not have had many strong ties to non-Black people, but they made effective use of the ties they had.

The upshot of our findings is that, consistent with Hypothesis 3, non-Black individuals were much more likely to protest due to ties with Black individuals than due to ties with non-Black individuals. This effect was particularly notable when the ties were strong, although strong ties are not necessary per se. What seems most important is the sharing of stories of harm by Black individuals in conversations.

6.5 Residential Integration

Hypothesis 3b predicts that non-Black folks living among Black neighbors will be more likely to protest. Table 9 shows the relationship between the

Encouragement to protest and sharing of racism stories

Percentage of respondents who recall their cross-cleavage ties encouraging protests and sharing stories about racism they had faced.

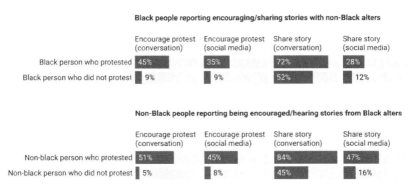

Figure 10 *Top*: Frequency with which Black people report sharing stories about racism with and encouraging non-Black alters to protest. *Bottom*: Frequency with which non-Black people report hearing these stories from and being encouraged by Black alters. Estimates are weighted to census benchmarks

Table 9 Probability of protest regressed on *Black pop share*. For additional results, see Online Appendix Table C9

Dependent Variable:			protest	
	Black		Non-Black	
Model:	(1)	(2)	(3)	(4)
Variables				
Black pop share	−0.006	−0.005	0.009**	0.009**
	(0.008)	(0.008)	(0.004)	(0.004)
Black favorability		0.008		0.03***
		(0.01)		(0.003)
ideological extremity		0.02***		0.02***
		(0.004)		(0.001)
covid		0.10***		0.05***
		(0.01)		(0.004)
Favorability (other races)		Yes		Yes
Demographic Controls	Yes	Yes	Yes	Yes
Fixed-effects				
state	Yes	Yes	Yes	Yes
wave	Yes	Yes	Yes	Yes
Fit statistics				
Observations	10,910	10,141	85,522	80,920
Squared Correlation	0.06202	0.08365	0.05280	0.07048
Pseudo R^2	0.17302	0.22319	−0.21744	−0.32767
BIC	4,147.4	3,941.2	−24,953.1	−22,878.1

Clustered (state) standard-errors in parentheses
*Signif. Codes: ***: 0.01, **: 0.05, *: 0.1*

respondent's decision to *protest* and the percentage of Black residents in the respondent's ZIP Code (*Black pop share*) (the measure we use for integration).[59] For Black respondents, the relationship between *Black pop share* and *protest* is negative and nonsignificant (Models 1–2). Thus, for Black individuals, the racial composition of their neighborhood does not influence protest decisions. In sharp contrast, the composition *does* matter for non-Black respondents. Specifically, the relationship for such individuals is positive and significant (Models 3–4). Moreover, it persists when controlling for respondents' feelings toward Black people (*Black favorability*) in Model 4. As we discuss in the next section, this means that it is indeed likely a residential effect (rather than some other socialization factor). The networks generated by their neighborhoods – Black networks – matter.[60]

To quantify this relationship, it is helpful to divide neighborhoods into "segregation quintiles" according to the percentage of residents who are Black. In the most segregated quintile – ZIP Codes where fewer than 1 in 200 residents is Black – only 2.8 percent of non-Black residents protested. In the least segregated quintile – ZIP Codes where over a third of residents are Black – 4.9 percent of non-Black residents protested (a 75 percent increase). This trend is confirmed when we regress non-Black turnout on the segregation quintiles, as shown in Online Appendix Table C10. Switching from the most segregated quintile to the least segregated increases the probability of non-Black protest by 1 percentage point, a 40 percent increase.

6.6 Alternative Explanations

The results in this section raise the question of why these particular non-Black individuals had cross-racial ties in the first place. Could some unobserved factor such as a social-justice-oriented upbringing have led them to befriend or live among Black people? Certainly. Could this underlying factor also drive protest participation without the help of cross-cleavage ties? Undoubtedly. Are such ties, therefore, merely a by-product of this underlying factor, with no impact of their own on protest participation? We find such an exclusion highly unlikely. Imagine, for instance, that a non-Black person's upbringing leads them to befriend many Black people and makes them more inclined to protest. Both causal relationships are almost certainly mediated by their feelings toward Black people (*Black favorability*). That is, the causal pathways include:

---

[59] We recognize there are other measures one could use; we use *Black pop share* since all else constant the presence of more Black residents increases the odds that a White resident will be influenced by a Black resident or networked to it, at some level.

[60] This coheres with work that accentuates the importance of geographic space in shaping political behavior (e.g., Enos 2017).

a. upbringing → *Black favorability* → friendships with Black people

b. upbringing → *Black favorability* → BLM protest

However, our main analyses in Tables 6–10 control for *Black favorability* in part to block the influence of upbringing and other unobserved factors from distorting our estimates of the effect of Black networks on protest.[61] While there may be other ways through which upbringing drives protest (e.g., an activist mentality), many of these are blocked (in part) by other controls such as *party* and *ideological extremity*. Furthermore, it is harder to imagine pathways through which upbringing would lead to friendships without affecting *Black favorability* along the way. One exception might be that upbringing leads people to live or work in places with a larger pool of potential Black friends. However, our models include *Black population share* and other ZIP Code features, as well as education and income, which tend to structure American social life (McPherson, Smith-Lovin, and Cook 2001). In sum, our model implies that among pairs of non-Black people who hold the same party preference and ideological extremity, fall in the same education and income brackets, live in similar ZIP Codes, and hold equally warm feelings toward Black people, the non-Black person with more ties to Black people is more likely to protest. This modeling strategy cannot completely rule out the influence of upbringing (or other factors) along additional pathways; indeed, in an observational study like this, no modeling strategy can remove all doubt. Nevertheless, the fact that cross-cleavage ties still contribute a "value added" to the probability of protest after other variables have been accounted for provides compelling evidence that Black networks *do* matter for non-Black turnout.

6.7 Implications

Perhaps the most extraordinary aspect of the summer 2020 BLM protests was that a majority of the protesters were not Black. This seems exceptional given that the protests emerged so quickly, despite the concomitant threat of COVID-19. In the prior section, we revealed how important social mobilization was to this process – notably, weak ties on social media as well as movement outsiders being mobilized by moral shocks. Missing from that story was the crucial role of Black networks.

---

[61] Indeed, *Black favorability* is strongly correlated with cross-cleavage ties. White respondents with no ties to Black people have a mean *Black favorability* rating of 68.5 (out of 100). For Whites with Black acquaintances (but not friends), the mean favorability was 76.9, while for Whites with Black friends, it was 84.1. This correlation suggests that *Black favorability* may indeed be capturing part of the reason why White people form (and maintain) ties with Black people. Conversely, it can imply that Black people motivate White friends to protest not only through latent feelings but through active recruitment and informational exposure. For instance, those with higher *Black favorability* are also more likely to report hearing friends' stories of victimization. Hearing such stories still exerts a significant effect, however, after *Black favorability* has been controlled for.

The results in this section make clear that the protests would not likely have occurred at the scale they did if not for the Black folks who shared stories of harm to mobilize non-Black individuals.

We saw evidence of the influence of Black networks on non-Black people at both the interpersonal and community levels. With regard to the former, decades of work explore whether intergroup contact affects the attitudes of those from an advantaged group. We move beyond this work by looking at how such contact can mobilize actual action. The more Black people with whom non-Black individuals communicated, the more likely they were to protest. These are cross-cleavage ties in action. We also add to work on intergroup contact by showing that the nature and content of that contact greatly matters. When individuals interact more with alters with whom they share strong ties, the effect is stronger. Moreover, in the case of these protests, learning about the harm that the marginalized group had faced was crucial. This occurred most often via personal storytelling. Theoretically, this suggests that all contact is not created equally and that to assess the impact of contact, one must account for the nature of the ties between those involved and the content of the contact. The findings also accentuate the power of narratives and how impactful it can be when those in vulnerable situations share their stories of harm. This helps to build coalitions of support. These individual stories may be particularly crucial given that generalized moral appeals tend to have less effect (e.g., English and Kalla 2021; Starck, Sinclair, and Shelton 2021).

Of course, not everyone will have intimate access to the stories of those who have experienced victimization. This is where our findings regarding cross-cleavage capital are crucial. Black networks can be built not only via interpersonal relationships but also in communities. In more integrated communities, we find non-Black people are more likely to protest. We suspect this is because such communities give those individuals access to stories of harm that they otherwise would not have heard, either directly from neighbors or through friends of friends.[62] This finding adds to work that shows the racial structure of neighborhoods can influence policymaking (e.g., Trounstine 2018). In this case, integrated communities contributed to the size of protests on behalf of Black victims. These protests, in turn, shifted media dialogues (Elmasry and el-Nawawy 2017; Leopold and Bell 2017), generated policy changes (see Ebbinghaus, Bailey, and Rubel 2021; Hanink and Dunbar 2022; Peay and McNair 2022) and electoral

---

[62] Alternatively, if Black are more likely to organized protests, then living near Black people may provide non-Black residents with more opportunities to attend a protest nearby. In either case, integrated neighborhoods result in more non-Black participation.

impacts (Teeselink and Melios 2021; but see Engist and Schafmeister 2022), and influenced racial attitudes (Dunivin et al., 2022).

While our findings paint a complex narrative about social mobilization through-out the Element, the bottom line is that the mobilization of non-Black protesters – who made up a majority of those who protested – could not have occurred without the outsized influence of Black individuals. While Black protesters were in the minority, the protests themselves occurred due to Black folks and the various paths through which they influenced others: Black networks mattered.

7 Conclusion: Where Do We Go from Here?

7.1 Summary of Findings

In this Element, we seek to join a spirited and ongoing conversation about how mass movements originate and develop. Some of our contributions pertain to the role of social networks in social movements in general and in the Black Lives Matter movement in particular. Despite decades of research on how tie strength affects political mobilization, the debate about the relative utility of "strong" and "weak" ties continues to turn up contradictory findings. Here, we have attempted to add clarity to this debate by differentiating three concepts that are frequently conflated in the protest literature – emotionally weak ties, ties linking insiders to outsiders, and cross-cleavage ties – and demonstrate that each has a distinct relationship to protest mobilization. First, while strong ties were frequently used to mobilize individuals through personal interactions, most protesters were not personally recruited. Instead, roughly half were mobilized through exposure to social media posts from people they knew – people who, on average, were not connected via strong ties and in fact seemed to be instead connected by emotion-ally weak ties. Second, despite a long literature on the importance of movement insiders recruiting family and friends, we find insiders had a far greater impact on mobilizing one another. Because insiders were more likely to be surrounded by a social milieu of other insiders, they were more likely to be motivated by household members, posts on social media, and the opportunity to socialize – and perhaps by peer pressure. Outsiders, in contrast, were more mobilized by bridges on lone individuals who lived farther afield and made direct one-on-one appeals. In particular, victims, regardless of their involvement in the movement, made major contributions to mobilizing outsiders.

Finally, we find substantial evidence that cross-cleavage capital – both on the community and individual level – helped drive non-Black protest turnout to record heights. Even though cross-cleavage social ties are both weaker and rarer in the United States than intra-racial ties, nearly half of non-Black protesters who reported someone encouraging them to protest said the person who encouraged them was Black. Black people also influenced their non-Black neighbors and friends, not merely through their personal recruitment but by sharing publicly their personal accounts of harm due to racism and police violence. Thus, Black Americans exercised considerable agency – where "agency" in this case implies that it was not just pre-existing ties but the ways that such ties were used – drawing on their cross-cleavage capital to mobilize their non-Black contacts.[63] Non-Black people were more likely to protest if they lived in proximity to more Black people, suggesting that diverse communities foster mutual assistance across racial lines. Intergroup contact, in addition to reducing prejudice, may in fact lead to political action on behalf of the oppressed outgroup.

7.2 Chaos or Community?

We use the section heading above to pay homage to Rev. Dr. Martin Luther King Jr.'s book, *Where Do We Go from Here: Chaos or Community?* (King 1967). In his final monograph, King considered the future of race relations in the wake of the civil rights movement: he worried that a post-civil-rights-movement nation would suffer more bloodshed at the hands of White racists and/or increasingly militant Black activists (chaos), and he hoped for a future marked by deeper unity across groups via radical reform (community).

The cross-racial findings regarding the role of group contact in BLM protest activity raise pertinent questions about the importance (and perils) of King's calls for "community" – and, more generally, about the trade-offs of harnessing a privileged group's political capital on behalf of the marginalized (see McAdam 1988). What are the implications of White participants outnumbering their Black colleagues in activities geared toward racial reform and justice for the latter? Does this suggest the real possibility of a more racially egalitarian society? Or does White sympathy exist only insofar as attention is galvanized to acts of official or extralegal White racial terror (e.g., killings by police officers and racist gunmen)? As W. E. B. Du Bois notes in *The Souls of Black Folk* (1903), the unfortunate historical reality is that Black people have frequently existed in the White imagination as objects of either contempt or pity, with the latter sentiment especially pronounced among White liberals, progressives, and self-described allies (Black 2007; Sanders and Ramasubramanian 2012; Scott 1997). If the trajectory of Black protest is moving in the direction of relying on appeals to White allyship mobilized through publicizing shocking acts of violence, will reliance on these allies narrow the movement's agenda? Will it

---

[63] To adopt the language of Pedulla and Pager (2019), Black Americans' success at mobilizing non-Black people in large numbers was due not merely to network placement (i.e., having a lot of cross-cleavage ties) but to network mobilization – that is, making the most of the ties they had.

hamper the capacity of a Black polity to build lasting organizational strength within their own communities?

These and related questions point to serious issues regarding the sometimes double-edged sword of White allyship: White mobilization in the service of racially progressive interests can be driven by genuine concern for alters, but it can also be driven by less savory motives like pity or virtue signaling. Nevertheless, it is hard to imagine overcoming racism – or any deep societal cleavage – without engaging both sides of the divide. Understanding this, Walton and other race scholars of social movements characterize a major priority of "Black politics" as building minority-majority coalitions (Walton, Smith, and Wallace 2017). Such coalition-building efforts need not be lasting (allies one day might be rivals the next), and they can definitely be fraught, particularly when allies have common interests but different priorities.[64] Black Lives Matter participants, with their vision of inclusiveness and their deft use of social media, have sought to meet the challenges of building coalitions head-on while maintaining a clear message (Merseth 2018; Mundt, Ross, and Burnett 2018; Ransby 2018; Roberts 2021). The evidence from our Element suggests that Black alters are not only keenly aware of how important it is to mobilize non-Black support for BLM but are also remarkably successful at doing so.

In addition to offering a way to explore the dynamics of the summer 2020 Black Lives Matter protests, this Element aims to call attention to weak ties, insider/outsider dynamics, and cross-cleavage capital as subjects for social movements scholars to further explore. For example, future work can further disentangle the important distinctions between mobilization and organization as pathways to civic action. Given the decentralized nature of the BLM protests and the lack of organizational influence on most participants, our findings may apply to other so-called "leaderless movements," including those in authoritarian states. In the absence of formal organizations, instigators of protests, strikes, and rebellions may still be able to mobilize millions of their fellow citizens through their weak and cross-cleavage ties. This is particularly important for marginalized groups seeking to rally allies to their cause. Residential integration may provide a bedrock of cross-cleavage capital that an oppressed minority can draw on, but integration will likely be even more effective in the presence of strong cross-cleavage ties through which majority group members can be exposed to the injustices that minorities face.

Mobilization of protesters via social media and cross-cleavage ties, however, might not necessarily result in effective change. A key question, as raised

---

[64] The challenges of coalition-building are a feature of all politics, not just in the United States, and certainly not only among its White and racial minority citizens.

eloquently by Tufekci (2014, 2017), is whether "leaderless movements" have the capacity for internal coordination and deliberation to deliver systematic pressure for policy change. The considerable organizational capacity and cadre of leadership of the civil rights movement was doing far more than mobilizing protests. Leaders had to negotiate inevitable divides within the movement, plot careful tactical moves to maximize impact, and lobby for policy change. This becomes even more difficult if such policy changes do not align with the interests of advantaged groups (Bell Jr. 1980; Carbado and Roithmayr 2014; Starck, Sinclair, and Shelton 2021).

We should also note that organizations may still have played an important role in creating the unseen infrastructure that protesters mobilized by family and friends remain unaware of. Our approach here focused on the immediate, personal networks of individual respondents, while network approaches that ask "who influenced the influencers" might find organizers and leaders at the origin of these webs of influence. In a sense, our study has focused on "last-mile mobilization," rather than the people who organized and initially publicized individual marches, vigils, and rallies. Future research should endeavor to connect this last-mile mobilization to its source. While it may be tempting to trace these lineages using Twitter data alone or by asking respondents which organizations they were members of, this study should serve as a caution to such approaches. A mobilizer who receives marching orders from an organization leader may recruit their best friend face to face, who then posts a picture on Instagram, which inspires a distant cross-cleavage acquaintance, and so forth. Only by studying multiple mobilization mechanisms together can we begin to understand how a society-wide social network shapes protest. In particular, in the absence of whole network data at the societal level, we might imagine approaches that track mobilization networks several steps away from the protesters (e.g., McGrady et al. 1995) to see if there are prolific but invisible influencers. We could also imagine a deep, qualitative exploration of how acts of cross-cleavage mobilization occurred – what was the catalyst for conversation across the divide?

7.3 A Sign of Things to Come?

We began this Element with a discussion of how unprecedented the summer of 2020 was in terms of protest mobilization. While exploring these unprecedented political events and dynamics, our overall findings suggest that protest organizers today can achieve mass participation without mass membership, relying on social media platforms and the social fabric of their society. These research discoveries provide insight into what leads some movements to evolve from concentrated local actions to massive, broad collective calls for change. As we demonstrate, movements have a better chance to garner substantial support by activating ties across groups, even if the activated ties are weak. Because these protests were so unique and the manner in which people mobilized went against some long-held conventional wisdom, it begs the question: Is this how things will happen from now on? Time will tell, but what our work makes clear is that it would be difficult to understand how networks will work in future social movements without isolating – and, in our case, reconsidering – how ties worked in the summer 2020 protests.

The year 2020 was a distinctive historical instant, a convergence of long-term sociological trends with a moment of acute epidemiological and political crisis. This moment was built over many decades of the evolving social networks of Americans (in part driven by a legal regime emerging from the 1960s) and centuries of injury. It was also built on the emergence of social media that have changed how we connect with our ties and, clearly, how quickly people can massively mobilize for protests. It was also a moment of peak frustration with the COVID-19 pandemic and with a president who regularly flirted with White nationalism. The moment notwithstanding, some of the distinct patterns of mobilization may be typical for the near-to-medium-term future because of those long-term societal changes. The structure of interracial ties is expected to evolve. The decline of organizational affiliation (Putnam 2000) and the rise of "networked individualism" (Rainie and Wellman 2012) seem unlikely to be reversed any time soon. The particular social media that were pre-eminent in 2020 may well decline and be replaced by others – for example, it is clear that Facebook is in significant decline among young people, and TikTok, WhatsApp, and others are on a rapid rise. But the capacity of social media to rapidly connect and mobilize through our (frequently interracial) weak ties suggests an enduring shift in the role that these ties play in mobilizing for protest.

The other enabling factor is a political culture in the United States that is generally friendly to speech and protest (Gause 2022c). As we ponder the future, one concern is over the ability of protests in general (and protests characterized by weak, outsider, and cross-cleavage ties in particular) to effect change in an increasingly anti-democratic political environment (e.g., Graham and Svolik 2020). As geopolitical shifts abroad and current events at home have confirmed, the possibility of an "illiberal turn" in the United States is more than just a talking point among pundits (Hoban 2018) or a thought experiment among social thinkers (e.g., Grumbach 2022). Evolving modes of protest mobilization are crucial for any citizens in democracies who want to come together against authoritarian threats. Conversely, hindering such collective action can undermine embattled democracies and reinforce autocratic regimes (King, Pan, and

Roberts 2013). Rather than suppressing online services and risking popular backlash (Hassanpour 2014; Roberts 2020), politicians with authoritarian proclivities could instead use social media and other platforms for propaganda (Woolley and Howard 2018) to foment racial, regional, or class polarization to "divide and conquer" nascent opposition movements (Tucker et al. 2017). The ability of the United States and other ethnically heterogeneous democracies to confront anti-democratic threats in the years ahead may therefore depend – at least, in part – on the maintenance of intergroup friendships and alliances that bridge social cleavages.

References

Adler, Paul S., and Seok-Woo Kwon. 2002. "Social Capital." *The Academy of Management Review* 27(1):17–40.

Alesina, Alberto, Edward Glaeser, and Bruce Sacerdote. 2001. "Why Doesn't the US Have a European-Style Welfare System?" Working Paper. *National Bureau of Economic Research*. https://doi.org/10.3386/w8524.

Allport, Gordon W. 1954. *The Nature of Prejudice*. Addison-Wesley.

Anderson, Benedict. 1983. *Imagined Communities*. Verso Books.

Andrasfay, Theresa, and Noreen Goldman. 2021. "Reductions in 2020 US Life Expectancy Due to COVID-19 and the Disproportionate Impact on the Black and Latino Populations." *Proceedings of the National Academy of Sciences* 118(5):e2014746118.

AP-NORC Center. 2020. "The June 2020 AP-NORC Center Poll." *The Association-NORC Center for Public Affairs Research*. https://apnorc.org/wp-content/uploads/2020/06/Topline_final_release5.pdf.

Arora, Maneesh. 2020. "Analysis: How the Coronavirus Pandemic Helped the Floyd Protests Become the Biggest in U.S. History." *Washington Post*, August 4. www.washingtonpost.com/politics/2020/08/05/how-coronavirus-pandemic-helped-floyd-protests-become-biggest-us-history/.

Arora, Maneesh, and Christopher T. Stout. 2019. "Letters for Black Lives." *Political Research Quarterly* 72(2):389–402.

Barroso, Amanda, and Rachel Minkin. 2020. "Recent protest attendees are more racially and ethnically diverse, younger than Americans overall. United States of America." Available at https://policycommons.net/artifacts/813321/recent-protest-attendees-are-more-racially-and-ethnically-diverse-younger-than-americans-overall/1686864/.

Bayes, Robin, James N. Druckman, Avery Goods, and Daniel C. Molden. 2020. "When and How Different Motives Can Drive Motivated Political Reasoning." *Political Psychology* 41(5):1031–52.

Bayes, Robin, James N. Druckman, and Alauna C. Safarpour. 2022. "Studying Science Inequities." *The Annals of the American Academy of Political and Social Science* 700(1):220–33.

Bell Jr. , Derrick A. 1980. "Brown v. Board of Education and the Interest-Convergence Dilemma." *Harvard Law Review* 93:518–33.

Bennett, W. Lance., and Alexandra Segerberg. 2012. "The Logic of Connective Action." *Information, Communication & Society* 15(5):739–68.

Black, Marc. 2007. "Fanon and DuBoisian Double Consciousness." *Human Architecture: Journal of the Sociology of Self-Knowledge* 5(3):393–404.

Blau, Peter M. 1993. "Multilevel Structural Analysis." *Social Networks* 15(2): 201–15.

Board, Marcus, Amber Spry, Shayla C. Nunnally, and Valeria Sinclair-Chapman. 2020. "Black Generational Politics and the Black Lives Matter Movement." *National Review of Black Politics* 1(4):452–73.

Bolsen, Toby, James N. Druckman, and Fay L. Cook. 2014. "The Influence of Partisan Motivated Reasoning on Public Opinion." *Political Behavior* 36(2):-235–62.

Bond, Robert M., Christopher J. Fariss, Jason J. Jones, et al. 2012. "A 61-Million-Person Experiment in Social Influence and Political Mobilization." *Nature* 489(7415):295–98.

Bonilla, Tabitha, and Alvin B. Tillery. 2020. "Which Identity Frames Boost Support for and Mobilization in the #BlackLivesMatter Movement?" *American Political Science Review* 114(4):947–62.

Boulianne, Shelley, and Sangwon Lee. 2022. "Conspiracy Beliefs, Misinformation, Social Media Platforms, and Protest Participation." *Media and Communication* 10(4):30–41.

Brashears, Matthew E., and Eric Quintane. 2018. "The Weakness of Tie Strength." *Social Networks* 55:104–15.

Broockman, David, and Joshua Kalla. 2016. "Durably Reducing Transphobia." *Science* 352(6282):220–24.

Brown, Jacob R., Ryan D. Enos, James Feigenbaum, and Soumyajit Mazumder. 2021. "Childhood Cross-Ethnic Exposure Predicts Political Behavior Seven Decades Later: Evidence from Linked Administrative Data." *Science Advances* 7(24):eabe8432.

Brown, Nadia E., Ray Block Jr., and Christopher Stout. 2020. *The Politics of Protest*. Routledge.

Browning, Rufus P., Dale R. Marshall, and David H. Tabb. 1984. *Protest Is Not Enough*. University of California Press.

Buchanan, Larry, Quoctrung Bui, and Jugal K. Patel. 2020. "Black Lives Matter May Be the Largest Movement in U.S. History." *The New York Times*, July 3. www.nytimes.com/interactive/2020/07/03/us/george-floyd-protests-crowd-size.html.

Bucher, Taina. 2012. "Want to Be on the Top?" *New Media & Society* 14(7): 1164–80.

Bunyasi, Tehama L., and Candis W. Smith. 2019. "Do All Black Lives Matter Equally to Black People?" *Journal of Race, Ethnicity, and Politics* 4(1):180–215.

Burke, Moira, and Robert E. Kraut. 2014. "Growing Closer on Facebook." *Proceedings of the SIGCHI Conference on Human Factors in Computing Systems* April:4187–96.

Burt, Ronald S. 2004. "Structural Holes and Good Ideas." *American Journal of Sociology* 110(2):349–99.

Campbell, David E., and Christina Wolbrecht. 2020. "The Resistance as Role Model." *Political Behavior* 42(4):1143–68.

Carbado, Devon W., and Daria Roithmayr. 2014. "Critical Race Theory Meets Social Science." *Annual Review of Law and Social Science* 10(1):149–67.

Carney, Nikita. 2016. "All Lives Matter, but So Does Race." *Humanity & Society* 40(2):180–99.

Castells, Manuel. 2015. *Networks of Outrage and Hope*. John Wiley.

Centola, Damon. 2010. "The Spread of Behavior in an Online Social Network Experiment." *Science* 329:1194–97.

Centola, Damon. 2018. *How Behavior Spreads*. Princeton University Press.

Checco, Monia D. 2018. "'Not Your Grandmamma's Civil Rights Movement'." *RSA Journal* 29:39–60.

Chenoweth, Erica, Barton H. Hamilton, Hedwig Lee, et al. 2022. "Who Protests, What Do They Protest, and Why?" Working Paper. *National Bureau of Economic Research*.

Chotiner, Isaac. 2020. "A Black Lives Matter Co-founder Explains Why This Time Is Different." *The New Yorker*, June 3. www.newyorker.com/news/q-and-a/a-black-lives-matter-co-founder-explains-why-this-time-is-different.

Cobb, Jelani. 2016. "The Matter of Black Lives." *The New Yorker*, March 6. www.newyorker.com/magazine/2016/03/14/where-is-black-lives-matter-headed.

Cohen, Cathy J., and Sarah J. Jackson. 2016. "Ask a Feminist." *Signs: Journal of Women in Culture and Society* 41(4):775–92.

Coleman, Eric, and Elinor Ostrom. 2011. "Experimental Contributions to Collective Action Theory." In *Cambridge Handbook of Experimental Political Science*, edited by James N. Druckman, Donald P. Green, James H. Kuklinski, and Arthur Lupia, 339–52 . Cambridge University Press.

Coleman, James S. 1988. "Social Capital in the Creation of Human Capital." *American Journal of Sociology* 94:95–120.

Costa, Mia. 2017. "How Responsive Are Political Elites?" *Journal of Experimental Political Science* 4(3):241–54.

Cox, Jonathan M. 2017. "The Source of a Movement." *Ethnic and Racial Studies* 40(11):1847–54.

Craig, Maureen A., and Jennifer A. Richeson. 2014. "More Diverse Yet Less Tolerant?" *Personality and Social Psychology Bulletin* 40(6):750–61.

Crisp, Richard J., and Rhiannon N. Turner. 2009. "Can Imagined Interactions Produce Positive Perceptions?" *American Psychologist* 64(4):231–40.

Crossley, Nick. 2002. *Making Sense of Social Movements*. McGraw-Hill Education.

Diani, Mario, and Doug McAdam. 2003. *Social Movements and Networks: Relational Approaches to Collective Action*. Oxford University Press.

Diekmann, Andreas. 1985. "Volunteer's Dilemma." *Journal of Conflict Resolution* 29(4):605–10.

Du Bois, W. E. B. 1903. *The Souls of Black Folk*. A. C. McClurg.

Dunivin, Zackary O., Harry Y. Yan, Jelani Ince, and Fabio Rojas. 2022. "Black Lives Matter Protests Shift Public Discourse." *Proceedings of the National Academy of Sciences* 119(10):e2117320119.

Earl, Jennifer, and Katrina Kimport. 2011. *Digitally Enabled Social Change*. MIT Press.

Ebbinghaus, Mathis, Nathan Bailey, and Jacob Rubel. 2021. "Defended or Defunded?" SocArXiv.

Edgar, Amanda N., and Andre E. Johnson. 2018. *The Struggle over Black Lives Matter and All Lives Matter*. Rowman & Littlefield.

Einav, Gali. 2022. "Media Reimagined." In *Transitioning Media in a Post COVID World: Digital Transformation, Immersive Technologies, and Consumer Behavior*, edited by Gali Einav, 19–28. Springer International.

Elmasry, Mohamad H., and Mohammed el-Nawawy. 2017. "Do Black Lives Matter?" *Journalism Practice* 11(7):857–75.

Engist, Oliver, and Felix Schafmeister. 2022. "Do Political Protests Mobilize Voters?" *Public Choice* 193(3):293–313.

English, Micah, and Joshua Kalla. 2021. "Racial Equality Frames and Public Policy Support." Working Paper. Yale University.

Enos, Ryan D. 2017. *The Space between Us*. Cambridge University Press.

Fishbein, Martin, and Icek Ajzen. 2009. *Predicting and Changing Behavior*. Psychology Press.

Fisher, Dana R. 2019. *American Resistance*. Columbia University Press.

Fisher, Dana R. 2020. "The Diversity of the Recent Black Lives Matter Protests Is a Good Sign for Racial Equity." *Brookings*, July 8. www.brookings.edu/blog/how-we-rise/2020/07/08/the-diversity-of-the-recent-black-lives-matter-protests-is-a-good-sign-for-racial-equity/.

Fisher, Dana R., and Stella M. Rouse. 2022. "Intersectionality within the Racial Justice Movement in the Summer of 2020." *Proceedings of the National Academy of Sciences* 119(30):e2118525119.

Fryer, Roland. 2007. "Guess Who's Been Coming to Dinner?" *Journal of Economic Perspectives* 21(2):71–90.

Fulmer, Sara M., Jan C. Frijters. 2009. "A Review of Self-Report and Alternative Approaches in the Measurement of Student Motivation." *Educational Psychology Review* 21:219–46.

Gamson, William A. 1992. *Talking Politics*. Cambridge University Press.

Garza, Alicia. 2021. *The Purpose of Power*. One World.

Gause, LaGina. 2022a. "Revealing Issue Salience via Costly Protest." *British Journal of Political Science* 52(1):259–79.

Gause, LaGina. 2022b. *The Advantage of Disadvantage*. Cambridge University Press.

Gause, LaGina. 2022c. "Costly Protest and Minority Representation in the United States." *PS: Political Science & Politics* 55(2):279–81.

Gee, Laura K., Jason Jones, and Moira Burke. 2017. "Social Networks and Labor Markets." *Journal of Labor Economics* 35(2):485–518.

Gelman, Andrew. 2008. "Scaling Regression Inputs by Dividing by Two Standard Deviations." *Statistics in Medicine* 27(15):2865–73.

Gelman, Andrew, and Yotam Margalit. 2021. "Social Penumbras Predict Political Attitudes." *Proceedings of the National Academy of Sciences* 118(6):e2019375118.

Gerber, Alan S., and Donald P. Green. 2000. "The Effects of Canvassing, Telephone Calls, and Direct Mail on Voter Turnout." *American Political Science Review* 94(3):653–63.

Gerber, Alan S., Donald P. Green, and Christopher W. Larimer. 2008. "Social Pressure and Voter Turnout." *American Political Science Review* 102(1):33–48.

Gould, Roger V. 2003. "Why Do Networks Matter?" In *Social Movements and Networks*, edited by Doug McAdam and Mario Diani, 233–57. Oxford University Press.

Graham, Matthew H., and Milan W. Svolik. 2020. "Democracy in America? Partisanship, Polarization, and the Robustness of Support for Democracy in the United States." *American Political Science Review* 114(2):392–409.

Granovetter, Mark S. 1973. "The Strength of Weak Ties." *American Journal of Sociology* 78(6):1360–80.

Green, Donald P., and Janelle S. Wong. 2009. "Tolerance and the Contact Hypothesis." In *The Political Psychology of Democratic Citizenship*, edited by Eugene Borgida, Christopher M. Federico, and John L. Sullivan, 228–46. Oxford University Press.

Green, Jon, James N. Druckman, Matthew A. Baum, et al. 2023. "Media Use and Vaccine Resistance." *PNAS Nexus* 2(5):146.

Green, Melanie C., and Timothy C. Brock. 2000. "The Role of Transportation in the Persuasiveness of Public Narratives." *Journal of Personality and Social Psychology* 79:701–21.

Green, Percy, Robin D. G. Kelley, Tef Poe, et al. 2016. "Generations of Struggle." *Transition* 119:9–16.

Groves, Robert M., Floyd J. Fowler Jr., Mick P. Couper, et al. 2009. *Survey Methodology.* 2nd ed. Wiley.

Grumbach, Jacob. 2022. *Laboratories against Democracy.* Princeton University Press.

Han, Hahrie, Elizabeth McKenna, and Michelle Oyakawa. 2021. *Prisms of the People.* The University of Chicago Press.

Hanink, Peter A., and Adam Dunbar. 2022. "Protesting the Police." *Social Movement Studies*:1–19. https://doi.org/10.1080/14742837.2022.2067842.

Hardin, Russell. 1982. *Collective Action.* Johns Hopkins University Press.

Hassanpour, Navid. 2014. "Media Disruption and Revolutionary Unrest." *Political Communication* 31(1):1–24.

Hässler, Tabea, Johannes Ullrich, Michelle Bernardino, et al. 2020. "A Large-Scale Test of the Link between Intergroup Contact and Support for Social Change." *Nature Human Behaviour* 4(4):380–86.

Heaney, Michael T. 2022. "Who Are Black Lives Matter Activists? Niche Realization in a Multimovement Environment." *Perspectives on Politics* 20(4): 1362–85.

Hillygus, D.Sunshine., and Todd G. Shields. 2009. *The Persuadable Voter.* Princeton University Press.

Hoban, Brennan. 2018. "The Rise of Illiberalism and How to Fight It." *Brookings*, September 21. www.brookings.edu/blog/brookings-now/2018/09/21/the-rise-of-illiberalism-and-how-to-fight-it/.

Imperial, Mark T. 2021. "Implementation Structures." *Oxford Research Encyclopedia of Politics.* https://doi.org/10.1093/acrefore/9780190228637.013.1750.

Jackson, Sarah J. 2016. "(Re)Imagining Intersectional Democracy from Black Feminism to Hashtag Activism." *Women's Studies in Communication* 39(4):-375–79.

Jackson, Sarah J., Moya Bailey, and Brooke F. Welles. 2020. *#HashtagActivism.* MIT Press.

Janfaza, Rachel. 2020. "TikTok Serves as Hub for #blacklivesmatter Activism: CNN Politics." *CNN*, June 4. www.cnn.com/2020/06/04/politics/tik-tok-black-lives-matter/index.html.

Jasper, James M., and Jane D. Poulsen. 1995. "Recruiting Strangers and Friends." *Social Problems* 42(4):493–512.

Jefferson, Hakeem. 2018. "Policing Norms." *SSRN Scholarly Paper.* https://papers.ssrn.com/abstract=3290862.

Jefferson, Hakeem. 2020. "The Curious Case of Black Conservatives: Construct Validity and the 7-point Liberal-Conservative Scale." Available at SSRN: https://ssrn.com/abstract=3602209 or http://dx.doi.org/10.2139/ssrn.3602209.

Kalla, Joshua L., and David E. Broockman. 2020. "Reducing Exclusionary Attitudes through Interpersonal Conversation." *American Political Science Review* 114(2):410–25.

Kalla, Joshua L., and David E. Broockman. 2023. "Which Narrative Strategies Durably Reduce Prejudice?" *American Journal of Political Science* 67(1):185–204.

King, Gary, Jennifer Pan, and Margaret E. Roberts. 2013. "How Censorship in China Allows Government Criticism but Silences Collective Expression." *American Political Science Review* 107(2):326–43.

King, Martin L. 1967. *Where Do We Go from Here?* Harper & Row.

Klandermans, Bert. 1984. "Mobilization and Participation." *American Sociological Review* 49(5):583–600.

Klandermans, Bert. 2004. "The Demand and Supply of Participation." In *The Blackwell Companion to Social Movements*, edited by David A. Snow, Sarah A. Soule, and Hanspeter Kriesi, 360–79. 1st ed. John Wiley.

Klandermans, Bert. 2015. "Motivations to Action." In *The Oxford Handbook of Social Movements*, edited by Donatella della Porta and Mario Diani, 219–30. Oxford University Press.

Kubin, Emily, Curtis Puryear, Chelsea Schein, and Kurt Gray. 2021. "Personal Experiences Bridge Moral and Political Divides Better than Facts." *Proceedings of the National Academy of Sciences* 118(6):e2008389118.

Kuran, Timur. 1991. "Now Out of Never." *World Politics* 44(1):7–48.

Larson, Jennifer M., Jonathan Nagler, Jonathan Ronen, and Joshua A. Tucker. 2019. "Social Networks and Protest Participation." *American Journal of Political Science* 63(3):690–705.

Lazer, David. 2022. "Why Counting Vaccinated Americans Doesn't Always Add Up." *Washington Post*, April 7. www.washingtonpost.com/politics/2022/04/07/covid-vaccinations-cdc-data/.

Lazer, David, Alexi Quintana, Ata Uslu, et al. 2023. "The COVID States Project #100: Estimating Current Vaccination Rates." *OSF Preprints*.

Lazer, David, Mauricio Santillana, Roy Perlis, et al. 2021. "The COVID States Project #10: The Pandemic and the Protests." *OSF Preprints*. https://osf.io/qw43g/download.

Lee, Taeku. 2002. *Mobilizing Public Opinion*. University of Chicago Press.

Leopold, Joy, and Myrtle P. Bell. 2017. "News Media and the Racialization of Protest." *Equality, Diversity and Inclusion: An International Journal* 36(8):720–35.

Lin, Nan. 1999. "Building a Network Theory of Social Capital." *Connections* 22(1):28–51.

Lipset, Seymour M., and Stein Rokkan. 1967. "Cleavage Structures, Party Systems, and Voter Alignments." In *Party Systems and Voter Alignments*, edited by Seymour M. Lipset and Stein Rokkan, 3–64. Free Press.

Literat, Ioana, and Neta Kligler-Vilenchik. 2019. "Youth Collective Political Expression on Social Media." *New Media & Society* 21(9):1988–2009.

Lohmann, Susanne. 1994. "The Dynamics of Informational Cascades." *World Politics* 47(1):42–101.

Lubbers, Miranda J., José L. Molina, and Hugo Valenzuela-García. 2019. "When Networks Speak Volumes." *Social Networks* 56:55–69.

Lubell, Mark, Sammy Zahran, and Arnold Vedlitz. 2007. "Collective Action and Citizen Responses to Global Warming." *Political Behavior* 29(3):391–413.

Lupia, Arthur, and Mathew D. McCubbins. 1998. *The Democratic Dilemma*. Cambridge University Press.

Marsden, Peter V. 1988. "Homogeneity in Confiding Relations." *Social Networks* 10(1):57–76.

Massey, Douglas S., and Nancy A. Denton. 2019. "American Apartheid: Segregation and the Making of the Underclass." In David Grusky, ed., *Social Stratification, Class, Race, and Gender in Sociological Perspective, Second Edition*. New York: Routledge, 660–70.

Mazumder, Soumyajit. 2019. "Black Lives Matter for Whites' Racial Prejudice." SocArXiv. https://doi.org/10.31235/osf.io/ap46d.

McAdam, Doug. 1986. "Recruitment to High-Risk Activism." *American Journal of Sociology* 92(1):64–90.

McAdam, Doug. 1988. *Freedom Summer*. Oxford University Press.

McAdam, Doug. 2010. *Political Process and the Development of Black Insurgency, 1930–1970*. University of Chicago Press.

McAdam, Doug. 2020. "We've Never Seen Protests Like These Before." *Jacobin*, June 20. https://jacobinmag.com/2020/06/george-floyd-protests-black-lives-matter-riots-demonstrations.

McAdam, Doug, John D. McCarthy, and Mayer N. Zald, eds. 1996. *Comparative Perspectives on Social Movements*. Cambridge University Press.

McAdam, Doug, Sidney Tarrow, and Charles Tilly. 2001. *Dynamics of Contention*. Cambridge University Press.

McCarthy, John D., and Mayer N. Zald. 1977. "Resource Mobilization and Social Movements." *American Journal of Sociology* 82(6):1212–41.

McClerking, Harwood K., and Tasha S. Philpot. 2008. "Struggling to Be Noticed." *PS: Political Science & Politics* 41(4):813–17.

McGlone, Peggy. 2016. "'This Ain't Yo Mama's Civil Rights Movement' T-shirt from Ferguson Donated to Smithsonian Museum." *Washington Post*, May 1. www.washingtonpost.com/news/arts-and-entertainment/wp/2016/03/01/this-aint-yo-mamas-civil-rights-movement-t-shirt-from-ferguson-donated-to-smithsonian/.

McGrady, Gene A., Clementine Marrow, Gail Myers, et al. 1995. "A Note on Implementation of a Random-Walk Design to Study Adolescent Social Networks." *Social Networks* 17(3):251–55.

McPherson, Miller, Lynn Smith-Lovin, and James M. Cook. 2001. "Birds of a Feather." *Annual Review of Sociology* 27(1):415–44.

Merseth, Julie L. 2018. "Race-ing Solidarity." *Politics, Groups, and Identities* 6(3):337–56.

Michener, Jamila. 2020. "Power from the Margins." *Urban Affairs Review* 56(5):1390–1422.

Miles, Eleanor, and Richard J. Crisp. 2014. "A Meta-Analytic Test of the Imagined Contact Hypothesis." *Group Processes & Intergroup Relations* 17(1):3–26.

Morris, Aldon. 1981. "Black Southern Student Sit-in Movement." *American Sociological Review* 46(6):744–67.

Morris, Aldon. 2000. "Reflections on Social Movement Theory." *Contemporary Sociology* 29(3):445–54.

Morris, Aldon. 2021. "From Civil Rights to Black Lives Matter." *Scientific American*. www.scientificamerican.com/report/the-black-lives-matter-move ment/.

Morris, Aldon, and Cedric Herring. 1987. "Theory and Research in Social Movements." In *Political Behavior Annual Volume 2*, edited by Samuel Long. Westview Press.

Mundt, Marcia, Karen Ross, and Charla M. Burnett. 2018. "Scaling Social Movements through Social Media." *Social Media + Society* 4(4):2056305 118807911. https://doi.org/10.1177/2056305118807911.

Nickerson, David W. 2008. "Is Voting Contagious?" *American Political Science Review* 102(1):49–57.

Oberschall, Anthony. 1973. *Social Conflict and Social Movements*. Pearson Education.

Olson, Mancur. 1965. *The Logic of Collective Action*. Harvard University Press.

Opp, Karl-Dieter, and Christiane Gern. 1993. "Dissident Groups, Personal Networks, and Spontaneous Cooperation." *American Sociological Review* 58(5):659–80.

Paluck, Elizabeth L., Seth A. Green, and Donald P. Green. 2019. "The Contact Hypothesis Re-evaluated." *Behavioural Public Policy* 3(2):129–58.

Parker, Kim, Juliana M. Horowitz, and Monica Anderson. 2020. "Majorities across Racial, Ethnic Groups Express Support for the Black Lives Matter Movement." *Pew Research Center's Social & Demographic Trends Project*, June 12. www.pewresearch.org/social-trends/2020/06/12/amid-protests-majorities-across-racial-and-ethnic-groups-express-support-for-the-black-lives-matter-movement/.

Parkinson, Sarah E. 2022. *Beyond the Lines*. Cornell University Press.

Passy, Florence. 2001. "Socialization, Connection, and the Structure/Agency Gap." *Mobilization: An International Quarterly* 6(2):173–92.

Peay, Periloux C., and Clinton R. McNair. 2022. "Concurrent Pressures of Mass Protests." *Politics, Groups, and Identities*. https://doi.org/10.1080/21565503.2022.2098148.

Pedulla, David S., and Devah Pager. 2019. "Race and Networks in the Job Search Process." *American Sociological Review* 84(6):983–1012.

Petrie, Michelle. 2004. "A Research Note on the Determinants of Protest Participation." *Sociological Spectrum* 24(5):553–74.

Pettigrew, Thomas F., and Linda R. Tropp. 2006. "A Meta-Analytic Test of Intergroup Contact Theory." *Journal of Personality and Social Psychology* 90(5):751–83.

Porta, Donatella della, and Mario Diani. 2020. *Social Movements*. John Wiley.

Putnam, Robert D. 2000. *Bowling Alone*. Simon and Schuster.

Quillian, Lincoln, Devah Pager, Ole Hexel, and Arnfinn H. Midtbøen. 2017. "Meta-Analysis of Field Experiments Shows No Change in Racial Discrimination in Hiring over Time." *Proceedings of the National Academy of Sciences* 114(41):10870–75.

Rainie, Lee, and Barry Wellman. 2012. *Networked*. MIT Press.

Rajkumar, Karthik, Guillaume Saint-Jacques, Iavor Bojinov, Erik Brynjolfsson, and Sinan Aral. 2022. "A Causal Test of the Strength of Weak Ties." *Science* 377(6612):1304–10.

Raleigh, Clionadh, Andrew Linke, Havard Hegre, and Joakim Karlsen. 2010. "Introducing ACLED." *Journal of Peace Research* 47(5):651–60.

Ransby, Barbara. 2018. *Making All Black Lives Matter*. University of California Press.

Ray, Rashawn, Melissa Brown, Neil Fraistat, and Edward Summers. 2017. "Ferguson and the Death of Michael Brown on Twitter." *Ethnic and Racial Studies* 40(11):1797–1813.

Roberts, Alaina E. 2021. "When Black Lives Matter Meets Indian Country." *The American Indian Quarterly* 45(3):250–71.

Roberts, Margaret E. 2020. "Resilience to Online Censorship." *Annual Review of Political Science* 23:401–19.

Roberts, Sam G. B., and Robin I. M. Dunbar. 2011. "Communication in Social Networks." *Personal Relationships* 18(3):439–52.

Rosenstone, Steven J., and John M. Hansen. 1993. *Mobilization, Participation, and Democracy in America*. Maxwell Macmillan International.

Ryn, Michelle V., and Jane Burke. 2000. "The Effect of Patient Race and Socio-economic Status on Physicians' Perceptions of Patients." *Social Science & Medicine* 50(6):813–28.

Sanders, Meghan S., and Srividya Ramasubramanian. 2012. "An Examination of African Americans' Stereotyped Perceptions of Fictional Media Characters." *Howard Journal of Communications* 23(1):17–39.

Schelling, Thomas C. 1960. *The Strategy of Conflict*. Harvard University Press.

Schultz, Alex, and Jay Parikh. 2020. "Keeping Our Services Stable and Reliable during the COVID-19 Outbreak." Corporate. *Meta Newsroom*, March 24. https://about.fb.com/news/2020/03/keeping-our-apps-stable-during-covid-19/.

Schussman, Alan, and Sara A. Soule. 2005. "Process and Protest." *Social Forces* 84(2):1083–1108.

Schwartz, Joseph E., and Peter M. Blau. 1997. *Crosscutting Social Circles: Testing a Macrostructural Theory of Intergroup Relations*. Routledge.

Scott, Daryl M. 1997. *Contempt and Pity*. University of North Carolina Press.

Shesterinina, Anastasia. 2021. *Mobilizing in Uncertainty*. Cornell University Press.

Shmargad, Yotam, and Samara Klar. 2020. "Sorting the News." *Political Communication* 37(3):423–46.

Simonson, Matthew D. 2021. "Cross-Cleavage Capital." Working Paper. Northeastern University.

Sinclair, Betsy. 2012. *The Social Citizen*. University of Chicago Press.

Small, Mario L. 2009. *Unanticipated Gains*. Oxford University Press.

Smith, Candis W., and Tehama L. Bunyasi. 2016. "The Influence of Black Lives Matter on Mainstreaming Intersectional Black Politics." *SSRN Scholarly Paper*. https://papers.ssrn.com/abstract=2845966.

Smith, Jeffrey A., Miller McPherson, and Lynn Smith-Lovin. 2014. "Social Distance in the United States." *American Sociological Review* 79(3):432–56.

Snow, David A., E. Burke. Rochford, Steven K. Worden, and Robert D. Benford. 1986. "Frame Alignment Processes, Micromobilization, and Movement Participation." *American Sociological Review* 51(4):464–81.

Staniland, Paul. 2014. *Networks of Rebellion*. Cornell University Press.

Starck, Jordan G., Stacey Sinclair, and J. Nicole. Shelton. 2021. "How University Diversity Rationales Inform Student Preferences and Outcomes." *Proceedings of the National Academy of Sciences* 118(16):e2013833118.

Steinert-Threlkeld, Zachary C. 2017. "Spontaneous Collective Action." *American Political Science Review* 111(2):379–403.

Stryker, Sheldon, Timothy J. Owens, and Robert W. White, eds. 2000. *Self, Identity, and Social Movements*. University of Minnesota Press.

Teeny, Jacob D., Joseph J. Siev, Pablo Briñol, and Richard E. Petty. 2021. "A Review and Conceptual Framework for Understanding Personalized Matching Effects in Persuasion." *Journal of Consumer Psychology* 31(2):382–414.

Teeselink, Bouke K., and Georgios Melios. 2021. "Weather to Protest." *SSRN Scholarly Paper*. https://doi.org/10.2139/ssrn.3809877.

Thompson, Debra. 2020. "The Intersectional Politics of Black Lives Matter." In *Turbulent Times, Transformational Possibilities?* edited by Fiona MacDonald and Alexandra Dobrowolsky, 368–87. University of Toronto Press.

Tilly, Charles. 1978. *From Mobilization to Revolution*. McGraw-Hill.

Tilly, Charles, and Lesley J. Wood. 2020. *Social Movements, 1768–2008*. 2nd ed. Routledge.

Tindall, David B. 2002. "Social Networks, Identification and Participation in an Environmental Movement." *Canadian Review of Sociology* 39(4):413–52.

Tindall, David B. 2015. "Networks as Constraints and Opportunities." In *Oxford Handbook of Social Movements*, edited by Donatella della Porta and Mario Diani, 231–45. Oxford University Press.

Tometi, Opal, and Gerald Lenoir. 2015. "Black Lives Matter Is Not a Civil Rights Movement." *Time*, December 10.

Tropp, Linda R., and Ozden Melis Uluğ. 2019. "Are White Women Showing Up for Racial Justice? Intergroup Contact, Closeness to People Targeted by Prejudice, and Collective Action." *Psychology of Women Quarterly* 43(3): 335–47.

Trounstine, Jessica. 2018. *Segregation by Design*. Cambridge University Press.

Tucker, Joshua A., Yannis Theocharis, Margaret E. Roberts, and Pablo Barberá. 2017. "From Liberation to Turmoil." *Journal of Democracy* 28(4):46–59.

Tufekci, Zeynep. 2014. "Social Movements and Governments in the Digital Age." *Journal of International Affairs* 68(1):1–18.

Tufekci, Zeynep. 2017. *Twitter and Tear Gas*. Yale University Press.

Valenzuela, Sebastián, Teresa Correa, and Homero G. de Zúñiga. 2018. "Ties, Likes, and Tweets." *Political Communication* 35(1):117–34.

Vehovar, Vasja, Vera Toepoel, and Stephanie Steinmetz. 2016. "Nonprobability Sampling." In *The SAGE Handbook of Survey Methodology*, 329–45. Vol. 1. Thousand Oaks, CA: Sage.

Verbeij, Tim, J. L. Pouwels, Ine Beyens, and Patti M. Valkenburg. 2022. "Experience Sampling Self-Reports of Social Media Use Have Comparable Predictive Validity to Digital Trace Measures." *Scientific Reports* 12(1):7611.

Vitak, Jessica, Nicole B. Ellison, and Charles Steinfield. 2011. "The Ties That Bond." *2011 44th Hawaii International Conference on System Sciences* February:1–10.

Walgrave, Stefaan, and Pauline Ketelaars. 2019. "The Recruitment Functions of Social Ties." *International Journal of Comparative Sociology* 60(5):301–23.

Walgrave, Stefaan, and Ruud Wouters. 2014. "The Missing Link in the Diffusion of Protest: Asking Others." *American Journal of Sociology* 119(60):1670–1709.

Walgrave, Stefaan, Ruud Wouters, and Pauline Ketelaars. 2022. "Mobilizing Usual versus Unusual Protesters." *The Sociological Quarterly* 63(1):48–73.

Walton, Hanes, Robert C. Smith, and Sherri L. Wallace. 2017. *American Politics and the African American Quest for Universal Freedom.* 8th ed. Routledge.

Washington, Jesse. 2020. "Why Did Black Lives Matter Protests Attract Unprecedented White Support?" *Andscape*, June 18. https://andscape.com/features/why-did-black-lives-matter-protests-attract-unprecedented-white-support/.

Wasow, Omar. 2020. "Agenda Seeding." *American Political Science Review* 114(3):638–59.

Whitaker, Stephan D. 2021. "Did the COVID-19 Pandemic Cause an Urban Exodus?" *Cleveland Fed District Data Brief* 20210205. https://doi.org/10.26509/frbc-ddb-20210205.

Wiltfang, Gregory L., and Doug McAdam. 1991. "The Costs and Risks of Social Activism." *Social Forces* 69(4):987–1010.

Wong, Leonard. 2003. *Why They Fight.* Strategic Studies Institute, U.S. Army War College.

Wood, Elisabeth J. 2003. *Insurgent Collective Action and Civil War in El Salvador.* Cambridge University Press.

Woolley, Samuel C., and Philip N. Howard. 2018. *Computational Propaganda.* Oxford University Press.

Woo-Yoo, Sung, and Homero Gil-de-Zúñiga. 2014. "Connecting Blog, Twitter and Facebook Use with Gaps in Knowledge and Participation." *Communication & Society* 27(4):33–48.

Zhao, Dingxin. 1998. "Ecologies of Social Movements." *American Journal of Sociology* 103(6):1493–1529.

Acknowledgments

We thank Matthew Baum, Jennifer Lin, Roy H. Perlis, Caroline Pippert, Hong Qu, Alauna Safarpour, Mauricio Santillana, Krissy Lunz Trujillo, and Ata Uslu for advice and assistance throughout. We thank Keith Gilyard, Marc Hetherington, Maryarita Kobotis, Clarence Lang, Anand Sokhey, Chagai Weiss, Michael West, and members of the Forum for the Study of Political Organizing and Collective Action for excellent comments. We also appreciate David Meyer and Suzanne Staggenborg for their guidance and input. We acknowledge financial support from the National Science Foundation under grants SES-2029292, SES-2029792, SES-2116465, SES-2116189, SES-2116458, SES-211663 as well as the John S. and James L. Knight Foundation, Amazon Web Services, and the Peter G. Peterson Foundation.

Cambridge Elements ≡

Contentious Politics

David S. Meyer
University of California, Irvine

David S. Meyer is Professor of Sociology and Political Science at the University of California, Irvine. He has written extensively on social movements and public policy, mostly in the United States, and is a winner of the John D. McCarthy Award for Lifetime Achievement in the Scholarship of Social Movements and Collective Behavior.

Suzanne Staggenborg
University of Pittsburgh

Suzanne Staggenborg is Professor of Sociology at the University of Pittsburgh. She has studied organizational and political dynamics in a variety of social movements, including the women's movement and the environmental movement, and is a winner of the John D. McCarthy Award for Lifetime Achievement in the Scholarship of Social Movements and Collective Behavior.

About the series

Cambridge Elements series in Contentious Politics provides an important opportunity to bridge research and communication about the politics of protest across disciplines and between the academy and a broader public. Our focus is on political engagement, disruption, and collective action that extends beyond the boundaries of conventional institutional politics. Social movements, revolutionary campaigns, organized reform efforts, and more or less spontaneous uprisings are the important and interesting developments that animate contemporary politics; we welcome studies and analyses that promote better understanding and dialogue.

Cambridge Elements ≡

Contentious Politics

Elements in the series

A full series listing is available at: www.cambridge.org/ECTP

Printed in the United States
by Baker & Taylor Publisher Services